Concepts of Recovery

The Journey

by
Concepts of Truth International Staff Writers:

Millie Lace, MSE, LPC
Pauly Bunting
Sherry Neuenschwander

special contribution by
Clint Saiben

Cover Design: Pam Gaskin, Wynne, AR 72396

Concepts of Truth International
PO Box 1438
Wynne, Arkansas

info@conceptsoftruth.org
www.conceptsoftruth.org
870.238.4329

ISBN-13: 978-0-9849652-1-2
The Library of Congress has cataloged the original edition as 2012941080.

Life is a Journey with different roads to travel; different places to visit; different ways of getting there whether walking, running or riding. This study will be the road less traveled, for abortion recovery is not easy. But this trip will be the adventure of a lifetime!

"Then you will know the truth, and the truth will set you free."
John 8:32

"I have personally reviewed Concepts of Truth International's abortion recovery curriculum Concepts of Recovery The Journey, and find it to be solid Christianly and clinically. This valuable, well-conceptualized and well-written resource no doubt will be a powerful agent of healing, growth, and redemption to many persons hurting from their intensely personal stories of shame and trauma. It expertly yet compassionately addresses the pain and pathos of post-abortion recovery both directly and deeply. I recommend it highly."

~ Jared Pingleton, Psy. D,
Director
Counseling Services
FocusOnTheFamily.com

"When a child dies it is always out of season. When a child dies, dreams die and we are all diminished by the loss of human potential. Although dying is a part of life, a child's death, in a very real sense, is unnatural and has a devastating and enduring impact."

(p. xv, IOM, 2003)

From the Director:

This recovery program is written in memory of the babies who have died from abortion and especially our daughter, Jill Allison Lace. It is for the mothers, fathers, sisters, brothers, aunts, uncles and all who are affected by abortion. Abortion affects as many lives as a single life could. I want to thank all of our staff at Concepts of Truth and the International Helpline for Abortion Recovery and Prevention for your tireless passion for this ministry. You all are a jewel in God's crown!

A special thanks to my husband Dail for all the years of unconditional love and support and especially for your patience with me during this project. Also, to staff writers Pauly Bunting and Sherry Neuenschwander, and Denise Mixson and Diane Pagan for editing; you are priceless! Thank you for your endless hours of hard work and in giving of your talent and creativity. A special thanks to Clint Saiben for writing A Man's Perspective. All in all, this book is for God's glory! May many be healed from the silent shame and pain of abortion, and may we all be a voice for the voiceless.

Millie Lace, MSE, LPC
Founder & Director of Concepts of Truth International

Testimonial

Healing is a journey, and with every step comes two choices to either stay where you are, or take the next courageous step further into the light. I am proud of you for choosing to take this step. There may be times, as you come to a pit stop of healing, that you may be hesitant and even scared to face some truths about your past abortion experience. Let me encourage you with these words, "you are NOT alone!" There are people who have been right where you are now who are praying for you and will be walking right beside you throughout this recovery process. You CAN find peace of mind after an abortion experience.

Whether elective, coerced, or forced, each abortion story is personal, and the pain is very real. No matter our culture, common threads of heartache, shame, guilt and hopelessness weave through each of our stories. In 1986, I had an abortion as result of rape. Someone from my past showed up at my door drunk. I was violated in every way imaginable, and the feelings that overwhelmed me I chose to ignore and to stuff them deep into my heart.

I had my second abortion within six months of my first one. I was so far into denial already, so the second one only seemed easier. Brad, my boyfriend at the time, went with me, and we made this decision together. Even though we have since married, the shame overtook us both, and we did not talk about it for years.

My shame increased because that same night after the second abortion, I ended up in the hospital with a fever and overwhelming pain due to an incomplete abortion and had to have a D&C. My heart sank and tears began to fall as I heard what the doctor said and reality set in . . . I killed my baby, I killed my children! The only children I will ever have are in heaven, because for them, I chose death instead of life!

But praise God, I know I have been forgiven! And it is by the grace of God that Brad and I are still together, and the fact that we both have gone through abortion recovery. In 2008 we attended a weekend retreat for couples offered by Concepts of Truth International. We are grateful for Dail and Millie Lace who walked beside us every step of the way! We now have come to accept what we have done, received forgiveness, and been able to move forward. Since then, God has opened many doors for me, including becoming a staff member of Concepts of Truth, working on the International Helpline for Abortion Recovery and Prevention. There is no greater joy than sharing truth with others and letting them know that recovery is available and possible.

I am thankful for this chance to work with Millie and Pauly on writing "*Concepts of Recovery The Journey,*" for it is another way that I can use my talents for the Kingdom of God. I give Him all the glory!

Sherry Neuenschwander, Marketing, Development & Staff Writer
Director of Spencerville, Ohio Office Concepts of Truth International

Contents

"Give sorrow words; the grief that does not speak,
Whispers the o'er-fraught heart and bids it break."

~ William Shakespeare

Introduction

Every journey begins with a single step. So it is true with the journey into your abortion experience. It may be a place you have visited often, or a place so hidden that you are not even sure how to find your way back. Whatever the case, please know that you are not alone on this journey. We will be with you every step of the way, helping you to navigate through this sometimes rocky and uneven road. Also, Jesus Christ will be our light, and He will illuminate each and every step and always catch us when we stumble.

I want to encourage you that at the end of this journey you will find great freedom. John 8:32 tells us that *"you will know the truth, and the truth will set you free."* This Bible study is about finding truth and dispelling the lies you have carried with you throughout your life. It is about helping you to understand that God is love and He wants to set you free. He loves you no matter what has happened in your past. This study will help you understand the grief surrounding abortion in the context of Biblical promises. I have found in my own life that Jesus knew exactly where I needed to be on my healing journey. For it is a journey not a destination. Every step you take simply leads you to the next step . . . the next area that needs His light to shine on it.

You will find that with every step on this journey of abortion recovery, instead of growing weaker, you will grow stronger. You began this journey with a heavy pack. It is loaded down with things like grief, denial, anger, unforgiveness, shame, guilt, perhaps depression, or loneliness. The truth is we all have things in our packs, each a little different, but still very much the same. On this journey we will be unpacking along the way. Leaving behind the things we no longer need and filling our pack with things that the Lord gives us. He is equipping us so that we may walk in freedom.

He promises in Isaiah 61:3 to give us joy for mourning, beauty for ashes, and strength for tears. You will experience all of this on this amazing journey of healing. Thank you for taking this step. The first step is always the hardest, and every step hereafter brings you closer to true freedom in Jesus.

Pauly Bunting, Staff Writer
Concepts of Truth International

A Man's Perspective

To the man who has had the strength to pick up this book and is starting the journey to freedom, I know this was not an easy step for you to take. John 15:5 says, "I am the vine; you are the branches. *If a man remains in me and I in him, he will bear much fruit; apart from me you can do nothing."*

This verse speaks to me through my own abortion experiences because I thought I had it all together, and I for sure didn't need the help. I thought I didn't need the help, and I especially didn't need a "healing weekend" or Bible study to talk about the whole thing!

In my teenage years I was part of two abortions. Whether you were like me and just let it happen, or maybe you didn't know that the abortion was happening until after the fact, or you forced someone into an abortion—we can't change the past. Know that the babies are with Jesus and have been okay from that very moment. Now we need to work on your healing so you can experience the freedom that God wants you to have and be ready to reunite with your child. I am going to ask you to trust me! If you're like me, this healing stuff is just for women, right? Wrong!

We are going to get to some uncomfortable spots on our journey together, and you'll just have to have the faith for now. You'll join me as I say, "It's worth it!"

Clint Saiben, Staff Writer
Ohio Concepts of Truth International

Chapter One
Where Am I?

Two things you must know when starting any journey, no matter your choice of navigation tools, is the starting point and destination. In this particular journey, that may be hard for you. If this is the first time you have looked at your abortion experience, then you may not quite be sure where you are starting. For those of you for whom it has been a constant companion, then you may feel you have a grasp on where to start. Either way, we want to let the Holy Spirit lead us in determining the areas in which we need healing. A decision to grieve an abortion is a search for God's heart and His redemptive purpose. So the first step in this journey starts with permission. Give yourself permission to grieve and heal. For all of us there is a grieving process that we go through in dealing with trauma and loss in our lives.

In abortion recovery the grief is "disenfranchised" since society has not allowed us to mourn. Disenfranchised means "deprived of a legal right or of some privilege or immunity." (Merriam-Webster Online Dictionary) Our grief then becomes complicated and layered with many facets, or grips, on our emotions and thinking systems. Responding to grief is as unique to an individual as one's fingerprints. One size does not fit all. This journey is uniquely yours, and yet we all process the same stages of grief according to Elizabeth Kubler-Ross. The stages are denial, anger, bargaining, depression, and finally acceptance. (Kubler-Ross, 1969)

In the loss of a child through elective or coerced abortion, **relief** often comes along as a traveling companion with the first stage of grief because the burden wasn't so much "a baby," but an unplanned pregnancy. So, in aborting our children, we are relieved of the pressures and/or hardship of a crisis pregnancy. A woman in an elective abortion might say, "*I'm so glad I'm not pregnant anymore.*" For men they may say, "*I'm glad I don't have that responsibility anymore.*" For someone who is coerced, for example if a woman feels pressure to not disgrace her family, she might say, "*I'm glad that is over, now I can move on.*" The family might say, "*I'm glad I was able to fix this for my daughter or wife or girlfriend.*" Relief often only lasts for a short time. When the reality of what you have really done, having or participating in an abortion, begins to settle, then denial takes over. If you were forced into an abortion, you probably did not experience relief because of feeling violated against your will, and you may have gone directly into denial to protect yourself from the reality of the trauma. **Denial** protects us from the pain of other emotions like anger and depression. Again, the length of time you are in each stage varies for each person. I know for me (Millie), it was 12 years of denial. I did not acknowledge my child as a "baby." I had been told that it was just tissue. I honestly didn't think I was taking a baby's life. I believed what I was told. The reality of taking a human life is too harsh for us so we sink into denial many times without even being consciously aware of this stage of grief.

Denial is hard to break, gets comfortable, and becomes home for us. We often live there so long that we forget we are in denial of any other reality.

Sometimes the encounter with the truth comes when you see pictures or models of fetal development and face the reality of how human your baby was, even early in development. It may come when you have a planned/wanted pregnancy and see the child as it develops, and then, when you hold it for the first time. It may happen when you turn to God and begin to seek after him, and he begins to show you truth in his Word that tears down the walls of denial in your life.

Moving from denial we may be fearful of the unknown and often become **angry**. We need someone to blame for this. It may be the clinic for not educating us enough about our choice. It may be the person that you felt forced or coerced you into the decision. For men they are often left with no choice or say in the decision. We are angry because we have a loss, we feel we have been wronged, and someone needs to pay for this. Anger can be expressed outwardly or inwardly. Either way it becomes a destructive force in our lives. To move from anger, one must forgive. We might say, "*If they admit the part they played in this, then I will forgive them.*" "*I want them to hurt as badly as I have hurt.*" We say these things because our loss is so great, and we need to know that someone is compensating for this loss. The problem with this thinking is, only Jesus can pay the price for sin. He paid it on the cross; and forgiveness, given or received, always starts at the cross.

Depression, with mixed feelings of anxiety or guilt, can be another stop on this journey. We often try and cope by justifying or rationalizing our behavior. We become very self-blaming, self-pitying and are unable to see past the circumstances of our life at the time of the abortion. We may also look to self-medicating options. Drug and alcohol abuse can come into play. We look for anything that can numb the pain we are feeling. Some people may use self-mutilation as a means to cope. Some may want to commit suicide. To move out of depression is to reach out to God and let go of our anger, bitterness, and unforgiveness. Many times we try bargaining with Him and others to try and reconcile the loss. But **forgiveness** is an important stop in this journey of healing, where we will start to remember events from God's perspective. We will unload the heaviness in our pack and pick up God's unconditional love.

The final stop on this journey is **acceptance**. It's looking at our past, our present, and our future with a sense of hope. It is being able to embrace who we are and step into God's blueprint of who He wants us to become. We know that even though our journey has been long and hard, it has caused us to grow, and we are now stronger for the remainder of the trip and our final destination. This comes about by accepting God's grace, allowing him to carry us, and walking it out in our daily lives.

Our staff writers at Concepts of Truth have all experienced the pain of abortion but have healed to help others. Every abortion experience has a unique set of circumstances surrounding the loss, but the commonality of the need to grieve the loss is the same.

Grief comes to us all; yet we carry it alone in our own way. On the International Helpline for Abortion Recovery and Prevention, we have heard from those hurting after abortion from ages 12-84. (Concepts of Truth) These include mothers, fathers, grandparents, and siblings; and even aunts, uncles, and close and distant friends. Abortion affects as many lives as a single life could.

We believe when processing the abortion experience you need a safe place to share. We are here to listen, give and receive feedback, pray, answer questions, lead you through tangible activities, and walk with you every step of the way. We encourage you to continue this healing journey to freedom, for this study will be one without minimizing, condemning, shaming, or confronting. This study is produced with love from those of us who have been there, so take courage . . . you are not alone!

The following questions will help you to know where you are on this journey and reveal to you just how abortion has affected your life. Prayerfully answer each question, allowing God to begin to shine his light on your soul.

1. What is your response when the abortion, and the circumstances around it, come to mind?

2. What reminders of the abortion(s) do you try to avoid?

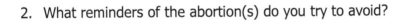

3. What feelings try to surface when you hear the word abortion or someone talking about it? What physical reactions do you have?
   Draw a picture that represents your feelings.

4. When reading through the chapter, where do you see yourself in the grieving process? (Note: it is normal to move back and forth between the various stages.)

5. Is there any person or persons that you have any strong negative emotions toward? For example, you may be angry toward a parent, sibling, the father or mother of the baby. Do you feel any of these individuals need to "pay" for their part in the abortion? If so, who?

6. Do you ever use any of the coping mechanisms that we mentioned earlier: justifying, rationalizing, alcohol, drugs, self-mutilation? If you do speak of the abortion, what emotions tend to begin to surface?

7. In what way do you feel the abortion has affected your interpersonal relationships? Do you struggle to get close to your children or others? Are you controlling, clingy and overly needy in your relationships? How has it affected your intimacy in relationships?

8. Think of prior life events that may have affected your thinking at the time of the abortion. Write on the timeline below positive and negative events in your life beginning with birth until today.

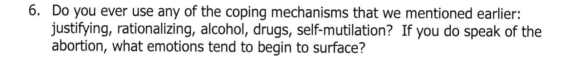

9. Do you struggle with denying yourself of anything or punishing yourself?

10. Describe how the abortion experience affected your relationship with God.

Truth for your Tank

"*To comfort all who mourn, and provide for those who grieve in Zion – to bestow on them a crown of beauty instead of ashes, the oil of joy instead of mourning, and a garment of praise instead of a spirit of despair.*" Isaiah 61:2b,3

Summary Question: Finish the following sentence: My goal for this healing journey is . . .

"All those years I fell for the great palace lie that grief should be gotten over as quickly as possible and as privately. But what I've discovered since is that the lifelong fear of grief keeps us in a barren, isolated place and that only grieving can heal grief."

~ Annie Lamott in "Traveling Mercies"

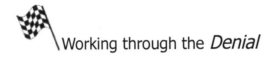
Working through the *Denial*

Identifying *Anger* toward him/herself and others involved

Forgiving Others

Dealing with *Depression* and the issues of guilt and shame

Accepting *God's Forgiveness* and *Forgiving Self*

Letting Go and grieving the loss

Acceptance–learning new ways to contend with the ongoing reminders and continuing the journey

Group Rules of the Road . . .

1. Confidentiality is assured by everyone, everywhere on the road, and with any turn along the way.

2. Commitment to full participation, completing lessons and attending group, able and willing to change, starting and ending on time.

3. Freedom to stop, turn around and leave, explaining the reason to the group. If participant does not have their own transportation they must provide an exit plan.

4. Non-judgmental.

5. Rescuing of other group members prohibits progress of the group; therefore, do not rescue others, or expect others to rescue.

6. Do not monopolize, interrupt, or give advice.

7. No sub-grouping; i.e., discussing the lesson with anyone before it is discussed with entire group.

8. Absolutely no mind-altering substances (other than prescribed medication).

9. As children of God, we agree on the essentials and will not criticize different denominations or doctrines.

10. Each group member will respect the individual differences of the healing journey.

CONTRACT/COMMITMENT FOR GROUP PARTICIPATION

(Please sign, tear out of book, and give this page to your group facilitator. Thanks!)

Those of us involved in the *Concepts of Recovery The Journey* weekend retreat are committed to help you in the healing process concerning your abortion experience, to listen and offer encouragement, and to keep every confidence. *This retreat will be facilitated by counselors who have been trained to facilitate post-abortion healing. They may or may not be licensed by the State. Therefore, this abortion recovery Bible study is not intended as a substitute for professional counseling.* Referrals will be made for professional counseling upon request or when considered appropriate by the facilitators of the Bible Study group. **The intention of the Abortion Recovery Bible Study is to help you understand grief issues in the context of biblical promises.** Because of the emotional nature of grieving, you can expect to feel angry, upset, and/or depressed as you work through your recovery. Facilitators must release information to each other and to current facilitator staff for the purpose of supervision and accountability. Data from the participant questionnaire may be used for research. Any information taken from this form will be used without your name attached to ensure your complete privacy.

There are certain circumstances in which we would be compelled to break confidentiality: 1) if we believe you are at risk for suicide, 2) if we believe there is abuse of a minor, or 3) if we believe you intend to harm another person or another person is intending to harm you.

I have read and understand the above._____(initial)

I promise to keep confidential the identity of others in the group and all personal information disclosed in the group._____(initial)

I promise to respect and value each group member and follow the group rules of the road._____(initial)

I voluntarily elect to attend the *Concepts of Recovery The Journey* retreat weekend sponsored by Concepts of Truth International, Wynne, Arkansas. _____(initial)

I release Concepts of Truth International, Wynne, Arkansas, its Board, employees and volunteers, from any claims for injuries or damages, physical or emotional, arising out of, or related to, my participation in the *Concepts of Recovery The Journey* retreat weekend. _____(initial)

_____   _____
Participant's Signature & Date   Printed Name & Address

                                        _____
                                        Facilitator's Name & Date

THINKING SYSTEMS AFTER ABORTION

According to Leigh F. Koerbel in *Fitting the Pieces Together*, 1997, "*Men often react differently from women to trauma in their lives. Women, after all, actually carried the baby in their wombs, whereas men were the more objective partner. However, God's answers to resolving abortion's spiritual and emotional aftermath are the same for both men and women. Therefore, it is crucial to **avoid** teaching post-abortive men that they have different needs from post-abortive women.*" (Koerbel, 1997)

The post-abortive man and woman has created and adopted a set of emotional and psychological defenses that have not allowed him or her to face the factual, emotional reality of his or her actions. This system of rationalizing is the basis for later emotional, psychological and relational problems. The rationalizing system begins its development the moment an individual considers abortion, it continues as they develop reasons to kill their child, and is complete at the moment the procedure is finished. The complete rationalizing system enables them to do what they have come to believe that they must do. The rationalizing system is designed to cover real emotional, psychological, and physical experience; distort facts and change reality to be consistent with his or her actions. (**Note:** This thinking system does not apply when abortion is forced.)

Two systems of thought and feeling are in conflict in the post-abortive man or woman. The rationalizing system is founded in the false assumption that life did not exist; and even if it did, his or her life is and was more important than the baby's life. The second thinking system, the system that represents facts, real experience and personal beliefs, is the system that is to be eradicated by the rationalizing system. In this system, it is the thinking, feeling, beliefs, values, and actions that have been unable to be expressed. This system carries the information that is contrary to the post-abortive man or woman's decision to abort. This system must be acknowledged in order for the guilt and shame to be resolved. The very existence of the guilt and shame is dependent on the conflict between what has become acceptable on a rationalized basis and what the actual experience of the post-abortive man or woman has been. Expression of the actual experience of the post-abortive man or woman is the critical issue in the resolution of the guilt and shame.

As the actual emotionally and psychologically traumatic experience of the post-abortive man or woman becomes more apparent, he or she becomes better able to regain control of his or her thinking, feelings, and actions. He or she now begins to "own," "accept" as real, the thoughts and feelings he or she has had to keep private or suppressed. The more he or she is able to express the intensely traumatic experience of the abortion and its aftermath, the better he or she feels, and the better he or she is able to cope. **This is not a new notion. An axiom of self-esteem development is as follows: the greater the personal honesty, the greater the self-esteem.** Facing facts and consequences of one's actions honestly adds to one's own personal integrity. The converse is also true. For the post-abortive man or woman, the adoption of this rationalizing system is to adopt a system of thinking and feeling and action that is by definition delusional and self-destructing.

THINKING SYSTEMS AFTER ABORTION (continued)

Social Institutional Response—Grieving is a natural and normal process for the post-abortive man or woman. He or she must be allowed to grieve and be supported and comforted in his or her loss. The need for the post-abortive man or woman to grieve is not supported within the present social institutions. In most cases of death, the survivor is afforded and generally encouraged to allow their sadness and loss to be experienced and expressed. The function of a funeral, wake, and church is to lend structure and process to the bereaved person. The basic institutions available to bereaved persons are not available to the post-abortive man or woman. The post-abortive man or woman is left to confront hostile social and institutional systems totally alone. He or she is left to deal with the death of his or her child in a complete social and institutional void. Family systems do not want to discuss the reality of the death of his or her child. They do not want to support the post-abortive man or woman in his or her grief. The family's focus becomes one of denial. The family reinforces and enables not talking, not communicating his or her abortion experience, and the concealing and suppressing of the facts and feelings related to the post-abortive man or woman's experience. The medical community is not in the least interested in dealing with or acknowledging the psychological and emotional consequences of their actions. This system is actually hostile to the post-abortive man or woman's need for access to him or her. The system's staff assume no responsibility for the psychological and emotional problems related to the abortion.

The funeral process is the major social and institutional mechanism by which grief is allowed to be experienced and expressed. Our culture has delegated to the funeral process this function. The post-abortive man or woman cannot enter this system because the death of his or her child has not been recognized as a social and/or personal reality.

A whole new methodology has to be enunciated to deal with the phenomena of Post-Abortion Trauma. It must include a new definition of the grieving process as it relates to the post-abortive man or woman's bereavement needs. This definition includes a rethinking and discussion of denial, anger, bargaining, guilt, shame, depression, and acceptance as these phases relate to the post-abortive man or woman's mourning process. (Terry Selby)

Reference:

Abortive Woman's Thinking System by Terry Selby, MSW, ACSW -Title and article modified to include men by Concepts of Truth International, 2008

Leigh F. Koerbel in *Fitting the Pieces Together*, 1997, P.A.M-Post *Abortive Ministries*

My Journey

My Journey

Chapter Two
The Map Maker

The map maker—the proper name is cartographer. (Merriam-Webster Online Dictionary) It's a person who designs maps and studies them. There is a God who has mapped out the world, the people and events, and the plan for your life. He loves you and has a plan, a road map for each of us. His target destination is relationship with Him. Then in that relationship together we navigate through life. Some may question his existence; some may know He is there but believe He doesn't really care about you or what happens to you; some see Him as a task master just waiting for you to make a wrong turn and then a giant hammer will beat you on the head and set you back on course. Some of you desire to walk in relationship with Him, but every time you take a step forward you feel that you then take five steps backward. Is there a God to whom we can bring all our hurts, doubts, questions, losses, and brokenness? Will He accept us with all of these things, or will He turn away from us? We want to look at the nature of God and who He is and how He wants to display Himself in our lives. When we can come face to face with His character and His attributes, then we can trust Him with all of the ugliness in our lives.

God as creator is seen in the first few chapters of Genesis. He spoke and things came to be. This world was empty, dark, and lifeless; and He spoke life into the formless void and made the beautiful world around us. He loved His creation and yet, with all the hosts of heaven, He still longed for a companion. He made Adam and Eve (us) in His image and walked with them in the cool of the day. God enjoyed their company and loved listening to them as they told him the things they had discovered each day. Imagine, if you will, Adam and Eve finding a beautiful waterfall and then describing it to the Lord. Of course God knew it was there for He created it, but God loved hearing the excitement in their voices as they told Him about it.

God didn't expect too much of Adam and Eve. He just gave them one rule: don't eat of the tree of the *Knowledge of Good and Evil*. Seems easy enough—one rule. God requires us to be totally dependent upon Him. We are His creation, and He longs for relationship with us. Satan tempts us with the pride of thinking we know more than God, or putting ourselves above God, just as he did before he was kicked out of heaven. So, God does not want us to make one decision without consulting Him first. Eve missed this one when she decided to eat of the fruit without checking with God first.

She has a moment of prideful, independent thinking. She thought it would be ok; she thought she could eat the fruit and nothing would happen; she thought perhaps God didn't quite know everything. Pride is the root of shame, so immediately after disobeying God, Adam and Eve are ashamed. Pride is what brings about the fruit of sin in our life. Most of us didn't include God in our abortion experience. If our abortion was elective or coerced, we thought we could fix it. We thought it was best. If we did pray it was a short prayer, and we tried to convince ourselves that it was ok. The fact is God knew what we were going to choose because He knows everything. Even in a forced abortion, God knew it was going to happen and He didn't stop it. This can be unsettling, yet God loved us so much that He gave us a free will to choose just like Adam and Eve. We can choose to love Him and to respond to him in obedience and bring our needs to Him. His Love is Changelessly Perfect. (Psalm 19:7) He Cannot Lie. (Numbers 23:19,20) **He is Omnipotent, Omnipresent and Omniscient. He is THE MAP MAKER!**

1. See Pg. 26. Read Genesis 1:26,27 and Genesis 3:1-13,23,24. What are your thoughts of God as creator? Being made unique in His image?

2. Sketch your family tree on the journal pages provided at the end of this chapter. List both positive and negative traits, "Blessings & Curses."
   Look for patterns of negative or positive traits in family relationships and/or behaviors. Sometimes "curses" are passed on to us spiritually through unconfessed sin. (Exodus 20:5,6) Was affection, trust, affirmation displayed or controlling, performing behaviors? Patterns of abuse or misfortune? Were there pseudo-secrets that kept you from learning about certain family members? Were you told you didn't need to know? We all have a "need to know" and a capacity to grow in the blueprint God has designed for us.

3. What areas of your life are you hiding from God? What areas of the abortion experience are you hiding?

4. There is a lady in the Bible who found herself very much in a crisis pregnancy situation. See Pg. 27. Read Genesis 16:1-16. To which feelings of hers (women) or Abraham's (men) can you relate? Name some things God would have seen or heard from you during this time.

Genesis 1:26,27

26 Then God said, "Let us make man in our image, in our likeness, and let them rule over the fish of the sea and the birds of the air, over the livestock, over all the earth,[b] and over all the creatures that move along the ground." 27So God created man in his own image, in the image of God he created him; male and female he created them.

Genesis 3: 1-13, 23, 24

3 Now the serpent was more crafty than any of the wild animals the LORD God had made. He said to the woman, "Did God really say, 'You must not eat from any tree in the garden'?" 2 The woman said to the serpent, "We may eat fruit from the trees in the garden, 3 but God did say, 'You must not eat fruit from the tree that is in the middle of the garden, and you must not touch it, or you will die.'" 4 "You will not surely die," the serpent said to the woman. 5 "For God knows that when you eat of it your eyes will be opened, and you will be like God, knowing good and evil." 6 When the woman saw that the fruit of the tree was good for food and pleasing to the eye, and also desirable for gaining wisdom, she took some and ate it. She also gave some to her husband, who was with her, and he ate it. 7 Then the eyes of both of them were opened, and they realized they were naked; so they sewed fig leaves together and made coverings for themselves. 8 Then the man and his wife heard the sound of the LORD God as he was walking in the garden in the cool of the day, and they hid from the LORD God among the trees of the garden. 9 But the LORD God called to the man, "Where are you?" 10 He answered, "I heard you in the garden, and I was afraid because I was naked; so I hid." 11 And he said, "Who told you that you were naked? Have you eaten from the tree that I commanded you not to eat from? " 12 The man said, "The woman you put here with me —she gave me some fruit from the tree, and I ate it." 13 Then the LORD God said to the woman, "What is this you have done?" The woman said, "The serpent deceived me, and I ate."

23 So the LORD God banished him from the Garden of Eden to work the ground from which he had been taken. 24 After he drove the man out, he placed on the east side[e] of the Garden of Eden cherubim and a flaming sword flashing back and forth to guard the way to the tree of life.

Genesis 16:1-16

[1] Now Sarai, Abram's wife, had borne him no children. But she had an Egyptian maidservant named Hagar; [2] so she said to Abram, "The LORD has kept me from having children. Go, sleep with my maidservant; perhaps I can build a family through her."

Abram agreed to what Sarai said. [3] So after Abram had been living in Canaan ten years, Sarai his wife took her Egyptian maidservant Hagar and gave her to her husband to be his wife. [4] He slept with Hagar, and she conceived.

When she knew she was pregnant, she began to despise her mistress. [5] Then Sarai said to Abram, "You are responsible for the wrong I am suffering. I put my servant in your arms, and now that she knows she is pregnant, she despises me. May the LORD judge between you and me."

[6] "Your servant is in your hands," Abram said. "Do with her whatever you think best." Then Sarai mistreated Hagar; so she fled from her.

[7] The angel of the LORD found Hagar near a spring in the desert; it was the spring that is beside the road to Shur. [8] And he said, "Hagar, servant of Sarai, where have you come from, and where are you going?"

"I'm running away from my mistress Sarai," she answered.

[9] Then the angel of the LORD told her, "Go back to your mistress and submit to her." [10] The angel added, "I will so increase your descendants that they will be too numerous to count."
[11] The angel of the LORD also said to her:

"You are now with child
    and you will have a son.
You shall name him Ishmael,[a]
    for the LORD has heard of your misery.
[12] He will be a wild donkey of a man;
    his hand will be against everyone
    and everyone's hand against him,
and he will live in hostility
    toward[b] all his brothers."

[13] She gave this name to the LORD who spoke to her: "You are the God who sees me," for she said, "I have now seen[c] the One who sees me." [14] That is why the well was called Beer Lahai Roi[d]; it is still there, between Kadesh and Bered.

[15] So Hagar bore Abram a son, and Abram gave the name Ishmael to the son she had borne. [16] Abram was eighty-six years old when Hagar bore him Ishmael.

Adam and Eve had to pay a price for their sin. Sin separates us from God. They were no longer allowed to be in the garden and enjoy the daily walks with their creator. We too suffer consequences for our sin. Abortion comes with many consequences, the greatest being the loss of our baby. God doesn't just leave us to fend for ourselves though. He is an all-knowing, all-powerful, all-seeing God who loves us and offers us a way to be in that daily walk with Him.

God wants us to grieve our losses and heal from the pain of abortion. He knows our thoughts, our actions, and desires. Nothing catches God by surprise. He knew the day you/ your girlfriend/wife/daughter would walk into that clinic. He knew the pain that would follow the moment you left. He knew the day you would be forced. He knew all the emotions you would feel. He bore our shame (Hebrews 12:2), and He promises in Hebrews 13:5 to never leave us or forsake us. He tells us in 2 Timothy 2:13, if we are faithless, He remains faithful. Psalms 139 speaks of how He intricately makes us and knows all our thoughts, and wherever we go we are still in His presence. God gave us free will, and He knows there are times in our life when we are going to exercise that right. Our choices, however wrong they are, never change how He feels about us. They never change the fact that He still wants to walk with us on this journey in the garden of life. Jeremiah 29:11,12 tells us that He has a plan for us to bring us a peace and a hope.

You may have experienced a forced abortion, abuse from your parents, or parents who didn't keep their promises, and that may have affected your ability to hold on to God's promises or believe they are for you. Force, abuse, and abortion dehumanizes us, but God wants to re-humanize us in our journey of healing. He reconciles the sins which He nailed on the cross. We are His creation, and God loves us more than our parents because God **IS LOVE**. (I John 4:8) We can call God "Abba Father" (Romans 8:14,15), and also know He nurtures us like a mother. (Isaiah 66:13)

5. How did you involve God in your abortion experience?
    What do you wish you had done differently?

6. Hebrews 12:5-11 says that God disciplines the ones He loves . . . us!
    Why is God's discipline to us important and why must He do it?

7. How is God like or not like your earthly father?

Christ Our Redeemer—Getting back on the map (in the garden) with God

Through the process of time, God knew that a sacrifice must be given for the sin of mankind. That one spotless lamb must take the sin of the world upon Himself, so that the relationship lost with Adam and Eve could be reinstated. God sent His only son Jesus to die for us. Jesus took our sin, every sin, even the sin of abortion to the cross. The price has been paid in full. We accept this forgiveness by believing that Jesus died for our sins, confessing our sins, believing in His redeeming grace and accepting Him as our Lord and Savior.

Sounds easy . . . it was not REALLY an easy thing. I (Pauly) felt that my abortion was too ugly, that I was such a terrible person that surely even God himself couldn't love me. I tried to work my way back to the cross. I served in the church, tried to make myself holy by following a list of do's and don'ts. It was a futile attempt. I could never perform well enough. I seemed to always be lacking no matter how hard I tried.

Then one day I realized that Jesus did the work on the cross. I began to understand that I am made holy and blameless because of the work He did on the cross, not by anything I could ever do. There is nothing I can do to make Him love me less or love me more. I am His creation! Wow! When I realized that, then I understood that I simply need to believe and depend on Him. No pressure, no measuring up. There is nothing we can do to make up for the sin of abortion. This knowledge must permeate our being, and we must accept God's grace as a free gift. Accepting God's grace doesn't mean we don't need to grieve our losses. It simply means we swallow our pride and don't put ourselves up above God. He is the great **I AM**. In John 8:57,58, scripture tells us that before Jesus was 50 years old, He had already seen Abraham! Wow! He **IS** the Great **I AM!** He is the **Alpha** and the **Omega**, the Beginning and the End! (Revelation 21:6)

8. Abortion is sin and sin separates us from God. If you were forced into an abortion, it is not your fault but is the sin of the perpetrator. Christ died as a payment for all sin. What does God promise to do for us according to 1 John 1:9? See Pg. 30.

9. See Pg. 30. Read Romans 10:9-13. Read Ephesians 2:4-10. What do you think about grace and God's forgiveness?

10. Can you accept that the grace of God is immeasurable and Jesus' work on the cross is payment for the sin of abortion? Why or why not?

I John 1:9

9 If we confess our sins, he is faithful and just and will forgive us our sins and purify us from all unrighteousness.

Romans 10:9-13

9 That if you confess with your mouth, "Jesus is Lord," and believe in your heart that God raised him from the dead, you will be saved. 10 For it is with your heart that you believe and are justified, and it is with your mouth that you confess and are saved. 11 As the Scripture says, "Anyone who trusts in him will never be put to shame."[a] 12 For there is no difference between Jew and Gentile —the same Lord is Lord of all and richly blesses all who call on him, 13 for, "Everyone who calls on the name of the Lord will be saved."[b]

Ephesians 2:4-10

4 But because of his great love for us, God, who is rich in mercy, 5 made us alive with Christ even when we were dead in transgressions —it is by grace you have been saved. 6 And God raised us up with Christ and seated us with him in the heavenly realms in Christ Jesus, 7 in order that in the coming ages he might show the incomparable riches of his grace, expressed in his kindness to us in Christ Jesus. 8 For it is by grace you have been saved, through faith —and this not from yourselves, it is the gift of God— 9 not by works, so that no one can boast. 10 For we are God's workmanship, created in Christ Jesus to do good works, which God prepared in advance for us to do.

Romans 5:18-21

[18] Consequently, just as the result of one trespass was condemnation for all men, so also the result of one act of righteousness was justification that brings life for all men. [19] For just as through the disobedience of the one man the many were made sinners, so also through the obedience of the one man the many will be made righteous. [20] The law was added so that the trespass might increase. But where sin increased, grace increased all the more, [21] so that, just as sin reigned in death, so also grace might reign through righteousness to bring eternal life through Jesus Christ our Lord.

Numbers 23:19

[19] God is not a man, that he should lie, nor a son of man, that he should change his mind. Does he speak and then not act? Does he promise and not fulfill?

Lamentations 3:22,23

[22] Because of the LORD's great love we are not consumed, for his compassions never fail.

2 Peter 3:9

[9] The Lord is not slow in keeping his promise, as some understand slowness. He is patient with you, not wanting anyone to perish, but everyone to come to repentance.

11. See Pg. 31. Read Romans 5:18-21 and write it out in your own words.

12. See Pg. 31. Read Numbers 23:19, Lamentations 3:22,23, and 2 Peter 3:9. Knowing the character of God can be healing and comforting to us. List the characteristics of God that never change and never fail.

13. Look at *The Map Maker* on the next page and see which name of God ministers to you the most. Then write a brief statement of how you see God working in your life in this way.

14. If you can't relate to any of the names of God as being currently active in your life, then pick one that you want to become real. Read the scripture and write a statement of what this would look like in your life's journey today.

15. List the persons who have been positive role models in your life. How has seeing them model Godly character helped you have a better understanding of the character of God?

THE MAP MAKER

John 1:1 says, "*In the beginning was the Word and the Word was with God and the Word was God.*" God reveals Himself unto us by the names He calls Himself in scripture. We begin to understand the nature of God as He is revealed to us through His word. On this journey of abortion recovery, we need a map maker; One who knows where we are going on our journey because He made the map and He made us! We long for One who understands us (Hebrews 2:14-18), and One who is even greater than our hearts (I John 3:20), that we can trust to never do us harm. When loss is processed through the eyes, nature, and character of God, truth is revealed. However, this is only possible through a relationship with Him. Then when truth is revealed, we are free to choose wisely, and even be given the strength to be a reflection of Him to the world. (Galatians 5:22,23) I (Millie) choose the Map Maker with the following names:

1. Elohim: My Creator (Genesis 1:1)

2. El Shaddai: God Almighty. El Shaddai is frequently used in the book of Job.
        (Job 40:1,2) (Lang)

3. El Elyon: Most high God.   Sovereign over all. (Genesis 14:18-20)

4. Adonai: My Lord, My Master. (Genesis 18:27)

5. Jehovah: Yahweh, the Great I AM. (Exodus 20:1-3)

6. Jehovah Jireh: The Lord will provide. God knew and supplied the needs of
        Abraham in the sacrifice of Issac. (Genesis 22:14)

7. Jehovah Rapha: The Lord who Heals. At the waters of Marah, God reveals
        Himself to the children of Israel as the Healer.
        (Exodus 15:22-26)

8. Jehovah Nissi: The Lord, our Banner. Moses built an altar and called it,
        The Lord is my Banner. (Exodus 17:14-16)

9. <u>Jehovah Mekeddeshem</u>: Lord Who Sanctifies. Sanctification, set apart to serve God. (Exodus 31:13) (I Thessalonians 5:23)

10. <u>Jehovah Shammah</u>: The Lord is there. The center of everything that happens. (Ezekiel 48:35)

11. <u>El Roi</u>: The God Who Sees. She (Hagar) gave this name to the Lord Who spoke to her, "*you are the God who sees me.*" (Genesis 16:13)

12. <u>Jehovah Shalom</u>: The Lord our Peace. God wants to be in a harmonious relationship with us—a perfect blending; as with the notes on a piano making beautiful music, not discordant. (Judges 6:24) (Romans 5:1)

(The Names of God Series)

See Yourself through God's Eyes!

Truth for your Tank
"*. . . Holy Father, protect them by the power of your name, the name you gave me, so that they may be one as we are one.*"   John 17:11b

Summary Question: What is holding you back in trusting the power of God to heal you from the pain of your abortion experience?

My Journey

My Journey

Chapter Three
Traveling Companions
Relief & Denial

"**A**hh, I'm not pregnant anymore, but oh, wait . . . what have I done!"

Remembering back to my abortion, I was so scared to be pregnant, but immediately afterward, I was in mental anguish. What had I done! Someone lined up for the cookies afterwards asked me if mine was a boy or girl! One would think that statement would have brought me out of denial, yet I pushed it back . . . surely I didn't kill a baby . . . after all . . . it is legal in this country! Plus, I had my family's support . . . I followed the doctor's advice . . . I had done the right thing!

But the lies begin to gnaw on our stomachs and in our hearts and minds if we have chosen an elective abortion or have yielded to the pressures of coercion. For me (Millie) it was 12 years of justifying and rationalizing what I had done.

Men tend to be fixers and protectors, and they believe that in helping a woman to choose abortion, they have fixed the problem and have protected her from a crisis situation. So there, the abortion fixed the problem and we find relief from it.

Relief is defined as: "alleviation, ease, or deliverance through the removal of pain, distress, oppression, etc., or a means or thing that relieves pain, distress, anxiety, etc." (Merriam-Webster Online Dictionary)

If the abortion was forced, there was probably not relief at all but total despair and helplessness and then denial of the trauma. If the abortion was elective or coerced, we were probably in a situation that was causing us pain and anxiety, and abortion removed the source of those feelings. **What we don't realize prior to having an abortion is, we are not alleviating pain or anxiety, but simply changing the source it is coming from.** Once we realize this, it is then too late to bring our babies back. Relief, then, is traded for denial. No longer can we look at what we have done or what we felt we had to do because the pain of finally realizing that abortion took the life of our child is too overwhelming. Many women have said, "*I just don't think about it*" or "*When thoughts of my abortion try to come out, I just push it back.*" Denial protects us from the reality of the trauma.

Relief and denial are ways of coping with loss, but they are also ways of responding to sin. Remembering the abortion seems too hard, so we stuff it down only to find that it is like trying to keep a balloon under water. It keeps coming up until we deal with it. And although men do not have abortions, they choose abortions. A sin is committed when someone willingly and knowingly chooses a moral wrong. Mothers, fathers, those who forced someone, and all who contributed to the abortion decision must confess the sin of abortion in order to heal from the pain.

Moving out of denial is one of the hardest things we face as post-abortive men and women. When we begin to see the reality of what we have done, it is often too painful. To move out of denial we must face head on the truth of our baby's humanity, and the truth of what abortion is. For me (Pauly) this was the hardest stage of grief to overcome. I was so accustomed to turning my feelings off, of redirecting my thoughts and silencing my pain that I had to learn how to have intentional thoughts and feelings. I had to come to a safe place (such as a Bible Study group), purposely look at reality, and allow myself to experience all the emotions that had been dammed up within my soul for years. It was a painful but necessary process for my healing, just as it is for yours. Defense mechanisms helped you to survive, but now it's time to face the past and begin the healing process. From a Christian perspective, these defense mechanisms guarded you from the truth. John 8:32 says, *"And then you will know the truth, and the truth will set you free!"* Your freedom is found by embracing the truth.

1. Was there ever a moment that you thought an inner voice tried to tell you that abortion was wrong? If yes, what did you tell yourself?

2. Many justify abortion by saying, "If abortion was wrong it wouldn't be legal." What does Proverbs 14:12 tell us? See Pg. 40.

3. Some of us convince ourselves that it was just a blob of tissue; it is often called "products of conception." See Pg. 40. Read Psalm 139:13-16. What does God see inside the womb?

Proverbs 14:12

12 There is a way that seems right to a man, but in the end it leads to death.

Psalm 139:13-16

13 For you created my inmost being; you knit me together in my mother's womb.
14 I praise you because I am fearfully and wonderfully made; your works are wonderful,
I know that full well. 15 My frame was not hidden from you when I was made in the
secret place. When I was woven together in the depths of the earth, 16 your eyes saw my
unformed body. All the days ordained for me were written in your book before one of them
came to be.

2 Samuel 11

[1] In the spring, at the time when kings go off to war, David sent Joab out with the king's men and the whole Israelite army. They destroyed the Ammonites and besieged Rabbah. But David remained in Jerusalem.[2] One evening David got up from his bed and walked around on the roof of the palace. From the roof he saw a woman bathing. The woman was very beautiful, [3] and David sent someone to find out about her. The man said, "Isn't this Bathsheba, the daughter of Eliam and the wife of Uriah the Hittite?" [4] Then David sent messengers to get her. She came to him, and he slept with her. (She had purified herself from her uncleanness.) Then[a] she went back home. [5] The woman conceived and sent word to David, saying, "I am pregnant."

[6] So David sent this word to Joab: "Send me Uriah the Hittite." And Joab sent him to David. [7] When Uriah came to him, David asked him how Joab was, how the soldiers were and how the war was going. [8] Then David said to Uriah, "Go down to your house and wash your feet." So Uriah left the palace, and a gift from the king was sent after him. [9] But Uriah slept at the entrance to the palace with all his master's servants and did not go down to his house.[10] When David was told, "Uriah did not go home," he asked him, "Haven't you just come from a distance? Why didn't you go home?"

[11] Uriah said to David, "The ark and Israel and Judah are staying in tents, and my master Joab and my lord's men are camped in the open fields. How could I go to my house to eat and drink and lie with my wife? As surely as you live, I will not do such a thing!" [12] Then David said to him, "Stay here one more day, and tomorrow I will send you back." So Uriah remained in Jerusalem that day and the next. [13] At David's invitation, he ate and drank with him, and David made him drunk. But in the evening Uriah went out to sleep on his mat among his master's servants; he did not go home. [14] In the morning David wrote a letter to Joab and sent it with Uriah. [15] In it he wrote, "Put Uriah in the front line where the fighting is fiercest. Then withdraw from him so he will be struck down and die." [16] So while Joab had the city under siege, he put Uriah at a place where he knew the strongest defenders were. [17] When the men of the city came out and fought against Joab, some of the men in David's army fell; moreover, Uriah the Hittite died. [18] Joab sent David a full account of the battle. [19] He instructed the messenger: "When you have finished giving the king this account of the battle, [20] the king's anger may flare up, and he may ask you, 'Why did you get so close to the city to fight? Didn't you know they would shoot arrows from the wall? [21] Who killed Abimelech son of Jerub-Besheth[b]? Didn't a woman throw an upper millstone on him from the wall, so that he died in Thebez? Why did you get so close to the wall?' If he asks you this, then say to him, 'Also, your servant Uriah the Hittite is dead.'" [22] The messenger set out, and when he arrived he told David everything Joab had sent him to say. [23] The messenger said to David, "The men overpowered us and came out against us in the open, but we drove them back to the entrance to the city gate.[24] Then the archers shot arrows at your servants from the wall, and some of the king's men died. Moreover, your servant Uriah the Hittite is dead." [25] David told the messenger, "Say this to Joab: 'Don't let this upset you; the sword devours one as well as another. Press the attack against the city and destroy it.' Say this to encourage Joab." [26] When Uriah's wife heard that her husband was dead, she mourned for him. [27] After the time of mourning was over, David had her brought to his house, and she became his wife and bore him a son. But the thing David had done displeased the LORD.

4. Some people tell us to leave the past in the past, or it happened years ago and there's no need to bring it up now. Psalm 90:8 says that God has our iniquities before Him and our secret sins are in the light of His presence. See Pg. 41. Read 2 Samuel 11. What was the problem David felt he had relieved when he had Uriah killed? Was there any sexual sin linked to your abortion experience?

5. Peter was trying to relieve himself of the pressures of the crowd by denying our Lord in Luke 22:54-62. Thinking back to the abortion experience, to what pressures where you responding? Or, if you were forced to what pressures do you think those forcing you were responding?

6. Facing the truth that abortion ended a human life is the only way to come out of denial and is the first step in grieving the loss. Finish the following statement: In order to deny my loss, I have always told myself . . .

7. Mothers and fathers share the responsibility of conceiving a child. What were yours and the father's (or mother's) thoughts and feelings once you knew of the pregnancy?

8. List date/s of abortion/s: # of weeks in pregnancy:
   Where did abortion occur?
   Father's name/s:
   List the persons who knew of the pregnancy and their responses:

9. The Bible is filled with examples of children who were foreknown before birth. Isaac, Ishmael, Jacob & Esau, Joseph, Samson, Job, Jeremiah & Jesus are examples. See Pg. 44. Read Luke 1:5-14. Who was the baby promised to Zacharias and what did he do in Luke 1:41-44 when Jesus' mother entered the room?

10. Women are natural nurturers of their children. See Pg. 44. Read Exodus 2:1-3. What did the mother of Moses do with him when Pharaoh ordered all males to be cast into the river?

11. In Malachi 4:6 (Hebrew text Malachi 3:24), God promises to turn the hearts of the fathers to their children. God gave men an innate ability to be protectors of children and the home. If you are the father of an aborted child, describe your feelings both past and present of not protecting your child or your child's mother during that experience. If you are the mother of an aborted child, write your feelings both past and present about your child's father.

12. Using the contribution pie diagram on page 45, how much of the decision to have an abortion was yours? How much responsibility can you give to others?

Divide the pie diagram into pieces (percentages), assigning anyone involved in the abortion decision their share. Don't forget to assign the abortionist, church, those who may have pressured or forced you, and society a piece of the pie.

Note: If you have had multiple abortion experiences, draw a pie for each one.

Luke 1:5-14

5 In the time of Herod king of Judea there was a priest named Zechariah, who belonged to the priestly division of Abijah; his wife Elizabeth was also a descendant of Aaron. 6 Both of them were upright in the sight of God, observing all the Lord's commandments and regulations blamelessly. 7 But they had no children, because Elizabeth was barren; and they were both well along in years.

8 Once when Zechariah's division was on duty and he was serving as priest before God, 9 he was chosen by lot, according to the custom of the priesthood, to go into the temple of the Lord and burn incense. 10 And when the time for the burning of incense came, all the assembled worshipers were praying outside.

11 Then an angel of the Lord appeared to him, standing at the right side of the altar of incense. 12 When Zechariah saw him, he was startled and was gripped with fear. 13 But the angel said to him: "Do not be afraid, Zechariah; your prayer has been heard. Your wife Elizabeth will bear you a son, and you are to give him the name John. 14 He will be a joy and delight to you, and many will rejoice because of his birth,

Luke 1: 41-44

41 When Elizabeth heard Mary's greeting, the baby leaped in her womb, and Elizabeth was filled with the Holy Spirit. 42 In a loud voice she exclaimed: "Blessed are you among women, and blessed is the child you will bear! 43 But why am I so favored, that the mother of my Lord should come to me? 44 As soon as the sound of your greeting reached my ears, the baby in my womb leaped for joy.

Exodus 2:1-3

1 Now a man of the house of Levi married a Levite woman, 2 and she became pregnant and gave birth to a son. When she saw that he was a fine child, she hid him for three months. 3 But when she could hide him no longer, she got a papyrus basket for him and coated it with tar and pitch. Then she placed the child in it and put it among the reeds along the bank of the Nile.

Contribution Pie

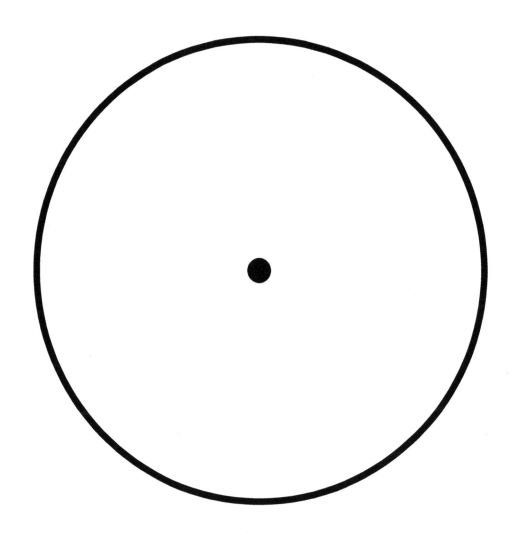

13. **Life Impact Timeline of Grief**

Starting with your earliest memory, list any major losses in your life from birth until today on the timeline below. These may include tangible or intangible things from special toys, career choices to a loss of a loved one, pet, loss of relationships with friends, family, etc. See my example first, then fill in your major losses on the second timeline. If you need more room than the space provided, feel free to use the extra space to draw an additional timeline.

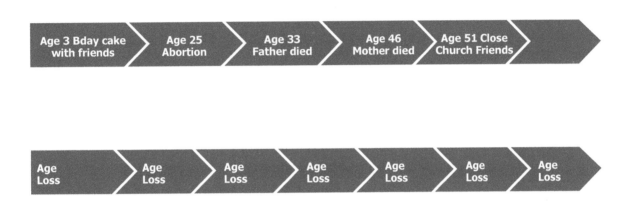

STRESS & DEFENSE MECHANISMS

Everyone has stress. It is unavoidable in our daily lives. Since we can't avoid it, we must learn to handle it in healthy ways. Think about a time when some bad stuff happened, but you were able to handle it since it didn't come too quickly, and you were able to deal with it before something else happened. For example, you may have experienced a parent being in the hospital, and then a child leaving home for college in the same year, but not at the same time.

Sometimes a lot of little stressors come all at once. This is very difficult to manage. At other times, one stressor such as an unplanned pregnancy, a pressured or forced abortion is so large that it can make us feel out of control and causes us to build up a defense for protection.

Defense mechanisms are personal strategies that we use when dealing with stressful situations. They protect us for a time; however, they only provide temporary relief to life's problems. Some common defense mechanisms are:

1. Repression–to have no consciousness of a painful or unacceptable occurrence in one's past. "I don't remember the abortion at all."

2. Suppression–to deliberately exclude from consciousness an emotion, occurrence, or idea. "I choose not to think about this." It is a conscious decision to push away the memory. A reminder triggered by sound, smell, dream, etc., is still pushed away.

3. Rationalization–to explain one's behavior by self-satisfying reasons, but not by the actual or unconscious reasons. "This is the best thing I could do because . . ." It is a justification for your behavior.

4. Total Denial–to refuse to believe, to disavow, or to contradict. "I never had any negative consequences to my abortion." "I never participated in any way in the abortion." Inability to face what has been done. Escape from a painful memory.

5. Minimizing–to deny the importance of what occurred. "I was told it was pregnancy tissue; everything will be okay." Minimizing is sometimes encouraged because other people don't want to talk about what really happened either.

6. Compensatory Pregnancy/Atonement Baby–try to become pregnant or impregnate another person to make up for the wrong. It is a deep desire to have another baby to replace, make up for, or fill empty arms.

7. Bargaining–Setting up conditions that must be met by others before a determined self action. "I will forgive the father or mother of the baby if he or she shows similar feelings of regret." Or "I'll forgive my parents when they show me that they care more about me than what others will think." The bargaining individual must realize he or she cannot change their past or change others.

8. Blaming–to place all responsibility on someone else. "I'm not responsible, they made me do it." "It was her decision."

9. Anger–to cover up true feelings (hurt, betrayal, sadness).

10. Avoidance–to stay away from pregnant women, babies, medical personnel, or physical exams so they won't trigger memories.

Prenatal Development of Human Life—First Nine Months (downloads/Heartlink)

2 Weeks/Conception day The egg and sperm most often unite in the fallopian tube (tube from the ovary to the uterus) to form a single cell called a zygote. This tiny new cell, smaller than a grain of salt, contains all the genetic information for every detail of the newly created life—the color of the hair and eyes, the intricate fine lines of the fingerprint, the physical appearance, the gender, the height and the skin tone.

Days 2–5 This new life is now called an embryo, and his or her cells continually divide while traveling down the fallopian tube before arriving at the uterus, around days 3 to 4. Meanwhile, the lining of the uterus prepares to receive this new life.

3 Weeks/Days 6–10 The embryo begins to implant in the lining of the uterus on about day 6. Once this occurs, hormones trigger the mother's body to nurture the pregnancy and prevent her monthly periods. Around day 8 the baby is about the size of the "period" used in this sentence.

4 Weeks/Week 2 A pregnancy test taken at this point can measure hCG, the pregnancy hormone in the mother's urine, and tell her if she is pregnant. By now, the embryo is completely attached to the lining of the uterus and draws nourishment from its mother.

5 Weeks The heart, about the size of a poppy seed, is the first organ to function—it begins beating just 21 days after fertilization! The first signs of brain development are evident and the foundation for every organ system is already established and beginning to develop.

6 Weeks Just 4 weeks after fertilization, the baby is growing rapidly and measures 1/8 of an inch long. The basic structure for the entire central nervous system (brain and spinal cord) has formed. The eyes are developing and the arm and leg buds are now visible. The heart is beating about 80 times a minute. An ultrasound can provide further medical confirmation of pregnancy.

7 Weeks The baby is now 1/3 of an inch long and his or her beating heart can be seen on a Doppler ultrasound. The embryo makes its own blood. The arm buds now look like tiny paddles, and the leg buds look like little flippers. Depending on the baby's gender, the testicles or ovaries are beginning to form.

8 Weeks The baby is now about 1/2 of an inch long from head to bottom. The elbows and fingers can be seen. Some reports show that the embryo can move its trunk and limbs and can respond to touch by reflex. Lungs begin to develop. Taste buds are forming on the tongue, tooth buds for "baby teeth" are taking shape in the jaw, and eyelids begin to form.

9 Weeks The baby measures 3/4 of an inch long and weighs almost 1/8 of an ounce. The developing ears and nose are visible, and there is pigment in the retina. Nipples can now be seen on the chest. The limbs and fingers are growing rapidly, and the bones in the arms begin to calcify and harden.

10 Weeks The baby's brain is growing rapidly. Each minute it produces almost 250,000 new neurons, and for the first time in development, the brain can make the muscles move on purpose. The upper and lower portions of the arms and legs are clearly seen, and the bony tissues of the legs begin to calcify. The fingers and toes are lengthening and are separate digits. By now the external ear is fully developed. A baby boy begins to produce the male hormone, testosterone.

11 Weeks Because the baby has all of the major organ systems and is a distinctly recognizable human being, he or she is no longer called an embryo but is now known as a fetus, a Latin word for "young one." The baby is about 2 inches long and can yawn and suck. The eyelids are fully formed and closed to protect the developing eyes. The intestines are developing and the kidneys begin to produce urine. During the next several weeks, his or her body will grow rapidly, increasing in weight 30 times and tripling in length in the next two months!

The heart begins to beat just **21 days after fertilization**, or **5 weeks** after the mother's last menstrual period began.

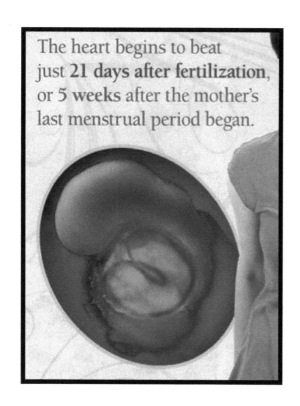

At **10 weeks**, for the first time in development, the brain can make the muscles move on purpose.

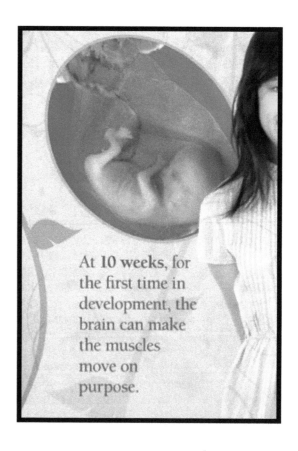

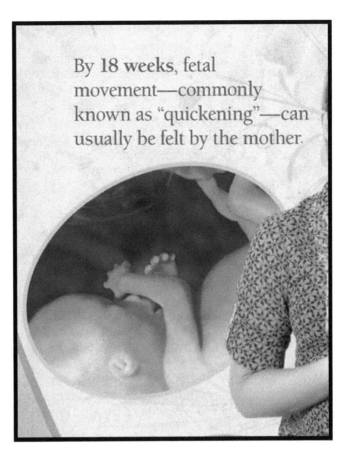

By **18 weeks**, fetal movement—commonly known as "quickening"—can usually be felt by the mother.

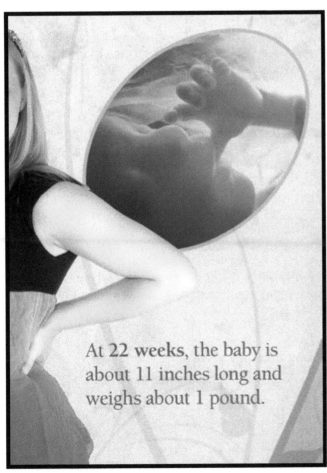

At **22 weeks**, the baby is about 11 inches long and weighs about 1 pound.

14 Weeks Now 3 1/2 inches long, the "young one" is coordinated enough to find his or her thumb and suck it. You can see the beginnings of the fingernails and toenails and the baby is able to urinate and swallow.

16 Weeks The heart beats between 110 and 180 times per minute and pumps about 25 quarts of blood each day. You can see the gender of the baby on ultrasound. If she is a girl, millions of eggs are now forming in her ovaries. At almost 5 inches in length and weighing nearly 4 ounces, the baby can coordinate the movement of its arms and legs, though his or her mother will not likely feel it yet.

18 Weeks In just 2 weeks, the fetus has almost doubled its weight to 7 ounces. The skeleton is hardening and calcifying and is visible on ultrasound. Reflexes such as blinking and frowning are now developed. The baby has its own unique fingerprints and toe prints. Some studies show that the baby can feel pain as early as 18 weeks.

20 Weeks The fetus is now about 10 inches long from head to heel and weighs 11 ounces. Fetal movement, commonly known as "quickening," can usually be felt by the mother. The baby has unique waking and sleeping patterns and even has a favorite position to sleep in. The pregnancy is about half over, and the mother is beginning "to show."

22 Weeks The baby is about 11 inches long and weighs about 1 pound. If the baby is male, his testicles are beginning to descend from the abdomen to the scrotum. Hair is visible on his or her head and body. From now until about 32 weeks, the baby feels pain more intensely than at any other time in development.

24 Weeks The baby now weighs about 1 1/2 pounds and inhales amniotic fluid in preparation for breathing. The ear has developed to the point where the baby recognizes his or her mother's voice, breathing and heartbeat. About a week ago, rapid eye movements began, an activity associated with dreaming. The baby may have a blink-startle response resulting from sound applied to the mother's abdomen. Some babies born at this stage of development are able to survive.

26 Weeks Now the baby weighs almost 2 pounds and he or she can react to sounds outside the mother's body. Eyes can now respond to light and the permanent teeth buds are apparent in the gums. Eyelashes and eyebrows are well-formed and the hair on the baby's head is growing longer.

28 Weeks The baby is now about 15 inches long and weighs about 2 1/2 pounds. With the support of intensive care, a baby born at this stage is capable of breathing air. The brain is developed enough to coordinate rhythmic breathing and regulate body temperature. As the baby continues to gain weight, the skin becomes less wrinkled and more smooth.

34 Weeks The baby is now about 17 inches long, weighs 4 1/2 pounds and continues to grow and mature. By this stage of development, the eyes are wide open, and if a light were shone into them, the pupils would constrict. The head is covered in hair, the fingernails have reached the tips of the fingers, and the toenails are close behind.

40 Weeks The baby is now around 20 inches long and may weigh 7 to 8 pounds. He or she has a plump body and a firm grasp. Typically, the baby is head down in the mother's pelvis and awaiting birth.

Truth for your Tank
"And then you will know the truth, and the truth will set you free." John 8:32

Summary Question: Relief and denial are used to cope with a loss. Finish the following sentence: When thinking of the abortion experience, I can no longer deny . . .

My Journey

My Journey

Along the Road

Robert Browning Hamilton

I walked a mile with Pleasure

She chattered all the way;

But left me none the wiser,

For all she had to say.

I walked a mile with Sorrow

And ne'er a word said she;

But, oh, the things I learned from her

When Sorrow walked with me!

"**D**ear God, I'm angry with the doctor for advising me to get an abortion. He hurt me (Millie) when he said my baby's heart wasn't beating yet."

I can remember writing that letter to God several years ago when I went through an abortion recovery group. I remember feeling odd writing a letter to God. Yet He created me. He knows all of my thoughts, feelings, hurts and losses, so why would I have a hard time sharing my innermost feelings with God? Well, for one, I didn't think I should be angry or had the right to be. After all, I was a Christian and I was taught that I "shouldn't" get angry. I know now that was false thinking and a roadblock to my healing. This was a false belief or roadblock that I had lived with for over 12 years. I know now that anger is a God-given emotion. And behind all anger is hurt, and behind hurt is loss. When we have a loss, we look for compensation.

Anger may be fueled by fear, frustration, and rejection. If I suppress my anger and do not process it, it will demand a response and come out in unhealthy ways at some of the most unexpected times and displaced on persons or things that do not have anything to do with the root of the anger. God wants us to bring any hurt or losses associated with our anger to Him, so what has been in the darkness will come to the light, and then He can heal it. Anger work has huge benefits in leading to spiritual and emotional health. Anyone who is influenced by parents to cut off, deny, and reject any feeling or expression of anger, will end up feeling emotionally constricted. If I deny myself of expressing anger, it can form roots of bitterness. It does not go away on its own.

Since God gave us the valuable emotion of anger, it is impossible to never be angry. Anyone who has been taught that anger is sinful and ugly will also come to believe that they are sinful and ugly because we cannot stop those feelings. Abortion leaves us feeling powerless, helpless, victimized, and voiceless. And typically, a man or woman who reacts to abortion this way is someone who was never encouraged, taught, or allowed earlier in life to find their voice and stand up for themselves.

Along this healing journey, it will be important to get around the roadblock of anger and leave the victim "stinkin' thinkin' " behind. We will need to rid ourselves of the false beliefs (the masks we wear), in which we have been accustomed, and adapt a "rebirth" of self in order to find our blueprint that God originally intended. When we know who we are in Christ and know how to stand for life and protect it, we will have the dignity of self God intended. Then and only then will we be able to have self-control and manage our anger.

Everyone from infancy on experiences angry feelings. These feelings are a part of the chemistry in our internal being that help people have the energy to be motivated to accomplish tasks, even difficult or threatening ones. In Genesis 1:28, God gave Adam and Eve an assigned task to maintain dominion over the earth. Adam and Eve had the capacity to be angry before the fall, but there was nothing to activate anger. Psalm 7:11 states, *"God is a righteous judge, a God who expresses His wrath or indignation every day."* The Bible makes it clear that anger is an ethically neutral instrument of force that can be used to motivate and not be used for sinful thoughts or behaviors. It has the potential for danger and can lead to sin. For those of us who regret our abortion experience, working through our anger is a major part of our grieving process. We may be angry with God, ourselves, and those whom we loved and trusted during the time of the abortion experience.

1. See Pg. 58. Read Ephesians 4:26,27. Is it possible to be angry and not sin? How?

2. List times that you have expressed your anger from a sinful nature. Also, list times you saw your parents angry and what it was like to be around them during that time.

If anger is held unchecked, rage can result. In Genesis 4:1-8 Cain killed Abel. The murder of Abel is indicative of what can happen when anger goes into rage. One can defile self and others. If we accept anger as a common part of life, it is imperative that we learn scriptural, practical, and healthy ways to make anger our servant. Once you are angry, you are in possession of energy which cannot be destroyed. Until you determine what form the expression of your energy will take, you have committed no sin. The moral challenge is this: We are responsible to determine what we will do with the energy our anger has created.

3. Hurting people hurt people. Once we believe that the actions of others against us were not right in God's eyes, we may feel justified to get even. What does Romans 12:19 say about getting even? See Pg. 58.

Ephesians 4:26, 27

26 "In your anger do not sin"[a]: Do not let the sun go down while you are still angry, 27 and do not give the devil a foothold.

Romans 12:19

19 Do not take revenge, my friends, but leave room for God's wrath, for it is written: "It is mine to avenge; I will repay,"[a] says the Lord.

I John 2:9-11

[9] Anyone who claims to be in the light but hates his brother is still in the darkness. [10] Whoever loves his brother lives in the light, and there is nothing in him[a] to make him stumble. [11] But whoever hates his brother is in the darkness and walks around in the darkness; he does not know where he is going, because the darkness has blinded him.

I John 1:6,7

[6] If we claim to have fellowship with him yet walk in the darkness, we lie and do not live by the truth. [7] But if we walk in the light, as he is in the light, we have fellowship with one another, and the blood of Jesus, his Son, purifies us from all[b] sin.

4. List anyone involved in your abortion experience with whom you are still angry.

5. Be honest with yourself, pray, and ask God to reveal any hidden anger from your abortion experience. Sketch a picture of the mask (if any) that you have been wearing to hide your anger and other true feelings.

6. See Pg. 59. Read I John 2:9-11. Describe what happens when we don't process our anger.

Anger involves our emotions and feels relatively safe. It's what triggered the anger that makes us feel vulnerable and at risk. We need to learn to trust God with our vulnerabilities. The surge of energy we feel in our body is processed through mental or cognitive (thought) processes. Whether we act out these strong feelings whenever anger occurs depends on our thoughts about the situation, ourselves, or others we see as stimulating our anger. Our belief about the situation, the threat we are facing, and how we have been taught to respond to anger can all affect our response. Since our thoughts are under our control (II Corinthians 10:4,5), anger can be controlled and become a servant and not a master of our life. Actually, it is people themselves who make themselves angry. Just think . . . we are our own roadblock! We must show ownership of our anger. See the Anger Cycle and ABC's of Behavior at the end of this chapter.

7. See Pg. 59. Read I John 1:6,7. What do we need to help us walk in this light and out of the darkness of anger?

8. Write a letter to God on the journal pages at the end of this chapter. Pray and be specific as to whom you may still be angry with about the abortion. List the ways this person(s) has hurt you. You may be angry with yourself for being an observer (standing by and allowing the abortion to happen) or perpetrating pain on your child through the abortion experience. Ask God to bring His light and help you process and heal your anger.

The Bible clearly states that we are to practice "*being slow to anger.*" (James 1:19) This simple admonition means we can work with angry feelings, not just bury them or release them in bursts of temper. We can learn how to take control, manage and utilize anger in productive ways.

When Ephesians 4 says to "*be angry and sin not,*" perhaps we should be urged to match our anger to that of Jesus, who was always looking out for the best interest of others and away from the source of all sin. The **I** in the middle of sin is our self-centeredness. Think about some of the times that Jesus expressed anger—in the synagogue when he healed the man with the withered hand he looked "*angrily*" at the Pharisees because they cared nothing for the man needing healing, only for their traditions and power. And when He expressed his anger toward the apostles, it was because they were preventing mothers from bringing children to Him to bless them. It was always on behalf of others. Whenever we are angry, it is usually because someone gets in our way.

To allow anger to motivate us to righteous and Godly living is for the good. To control the anger by holding it in and releasing it slowly, as the Bible states, or letting it go without hurting ourselves or others, is more emotionally helpful and healthy.

9. Read the sentences below and mark each with a (P) for Positive and (N) for negative to describe the result indicated.

_____ Anger brings about needed change (good change).

_____ Anger brings resentment and bitterness when internalized.

_____ Anger can make an impression for truth (we get honest).

_____ Anger sometimes becomes a habit.

_____ Anger can be a vent that keeps us from facing the real issue.

_____ Anger is a strong motivator.

_____ Anger can be used to rebuke and/or correct.

_____ Anger produces walls that keep us from growing.

Anger is a choice. We must decide what we are going to do with it. Unresolved anger can become a driving force in our lives. Do we want to stay mad using justification, and do we enjoy our anger by feeling that it gives us control? Ask God to help you remove the road-block of anger and to use it for wholeness in your life, not destruction. See Pg. 62. Read Ephesians 4:32.

10. List below any conscious effort you are making to take off your mask and learn from your anger.

Ephesians 4:32

[32] Be kind and compassionate to one another, forgiving each other, just as in Christ God forgave you.

Anger Cycle & ABC'S of Behavior
There are many points of escape in the progression of anger.

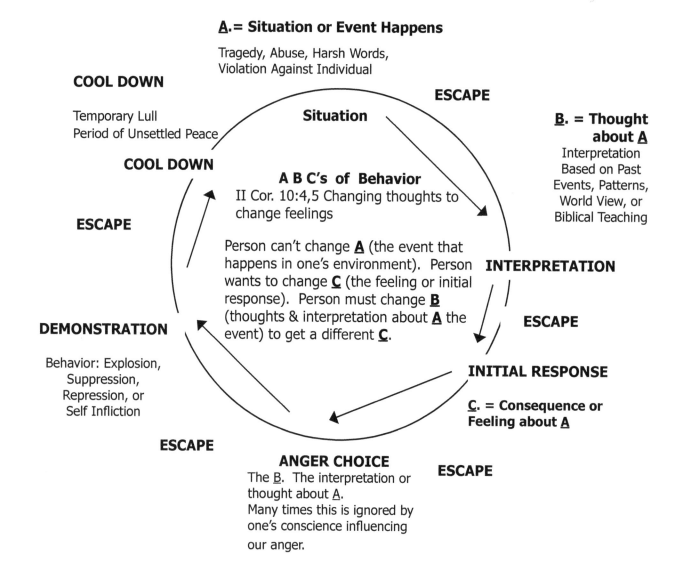

A.= Situation or Event Happens

Tragedy, Abuse, Harsh Words,
Violation Against Individual

COOL DOWN

Temporary Lull
Period of Unsettled Peace

COOL DOWN

ESCAPE

Situation

ESCAPE

B. = Thought about A
Interpretation
Based on Past
Events, Patterns,
World View, or
Biblical Teaching

A B C's of Behavior
II Cor. 10:4,5 Changing thoughts to
change feelings

Person can't change **A** (the event that
happens in one's environment). Person
wants to change **C** (the feeling or initial
response). Person must change **B**
(thoughts & interpretation about **A** the
event) to get a different **C**.

INTERPRETATION

ESCAPE

DEMONSTRATION

Behavior: Explosion,
Suppression,
Repression, or
Self Infliction

INITIAL RESPONSE

**C. = Consequence or
Feeling about A**

ESCAPE

ANGER CHOICE
The B. The interpretation or
thought about A.
Many times this is ignored by
one's conscience influencing
our anger.

ESCAPE

Escape Routes:
- ❖ **Time Out**   Remove yourself temporarily from the situation.
- ❖ **Identify Emotional Patterns** How do you typically respond to particular situations?
- ❖ **Journaling** Record each situation and your response to it.
- ❖ **Identify Primary Feeling** If anger is secondary, what feeling is causing this anger?
- ❖ **Analysis** Think - What led to this feeling? What is the root? What is a lie of the enemy?
- ❖ **Calming Techniques** Breathe deeply. Go for a walk. Pray.
- ❖ **Self Care** Take time for yourself. Eat properly. Exercise. Take time with the Lord.
- ❖ **Self Talk** Talk yourself through more positive interpretation. Recall God's truths.
- ❖ **Prayer** Ask God.
- ❖ **Contracting** Commitment to walk through this process before reacting.
- ❖ **Listen** to other person's point of view.
- ❖ **Support** from someone you trust . . . family, friend, counselor, support group.

Truth for your Tank
"Better a patient man than a warrior, a man who controls his temper than one who takes a city." Proverbs 16:32

Summary Question: Finish the following sentence. Anger is . . .

My Journey

My Journey

"Grief is healed when we are able to courageously stand in it and not run. When we are able to name it and start to know its comings and goings. When we are able to slow down our pace and find a place to experience our pain within. When we are able to be in our body. When we are able to accept it as a temporary visitor and not think that we are that grief. When are able to make an agreement with the part of ourselves that is the mask self, in order to access our pain. And when we can discriminate between the pain of grief and the pain of pain."

~ Thomas R. Golden

Chapter Five
Taking Forgiveness by the Hand

In the book, *Search for Significance*, author Robert S. McGee writes, "*The modern idea of forgiveness is to approach an offense with a large eraser and wipe it off the books. God has never forgiven like this. For each offense, He demanded full payment. This is the reason for the cross. Beside every offense on our ledger is the blood of Christ, which has paid for our sins in full.*" (McGee, 1990 2nd Edition) I'll take that! I (Millie) think it is a good idea to take forgiveness by the hand on this journey of abortion recovery. What? Forgiveness for abortion? Oh no, not that sin. Maybe all of my other sins, but surely God couldn't forgive me or those who have forced abortion on others for that horrible murder of another human being.

But yes, the sin debt is paid in full! (John 3:16) **Ahh! The unconditional love of God.** Not only does God provide forgiveness by giving His only Son, Jesus Christ on the cross; but as Linda Cochrane, my friend so eloquently says, "*the idea of forgiveness originated with him!*" God provided it for us . . . a people who were bound to fail but would want to return to Him to seek his mercy and forgiveness. I learned a long time ago that forgiveness does not equal trust; and forgiveness is not an eraser! None of us are above falling for deception, failing, wanting mercy, and coming back to God for forgiveness again. Even those we can forgive can hurt us again. So, just because I forgive someone for wronging me doesn't mean I can trust them to never hurt me again. And I must realize that forgiveness is not reconciliation. Only God can settle the debt of a repentant heart. But because we are forgiven much, we love much. (Luke 7:47) We have peace once we have been forgiven; so it is when we forgive others, a burden will be lifted. John 10:10 says that the thief comes only to steal, kill, and destroy, but Christ has come that I might have life and have it to the full. Matthew 6:14,15 says, "*For if you forgive men when they sin against you, your heavenly Father will also forgive you. But if you do not forgive men their sins, your Father will not forgive your sins.*"

So maybe I can finally forgive those involved in the abortion decision, but how can I ever forgive myself ?

Through the years I have heard differing opinions about forgiving self. Some get into theological debates about us having no power to forgive ourselves. And truly, only God, through His son Jesus' death on the cross and his shed blood has the power to forgive. (I John 1:9) And, we must have a repentant heart. But if I am refusing to accept God's forgiveness for the sin of abortion, then I am putting myself up above God! I don't think any of us want to do that. So, now do you get it? We must **Accept** God's forgiveness. That is easier said than done. Because when we truly **Accept** God's forgiveness for the sin of abortion, then and only then will we be able to forgive ourselves. We will give up the unforgiveness from our power and possession and let it go free all the way to the cross of Calvary. That, my friend is how we forgive ourselves! But remember, we are on a journey and forgiveness is a process.

1. See Pg. 70. Read I John 1:9. What is the first step of forgiveness from God?

Our sins need to be reconciled to God. Whether Catholic or Protestant, it is important to confess the sin of abortion to a minister or priest. This does not mean we do not **also** confess our sins to God directly. The sacrament of reconciliation is Christ's gift to us. The root of all sin is pride; its antidote is humility; confessing one's sins to God's appointed representative calls for tremendous humility. The priest, presbyter, or minister does not act on his own; He acts in the name of God and on behalf of His Church, administering God's forgiveness (absolution). The shame of abortion that silences us from confessing one to another is a root of pride, and this gives the enemy a stronghold on our victory through Christ. James 5:15-17 says, "*Therefore confess your sins to each other and pray for each other so that you may be healed . . .*"

2. See Pg. 70. Read *The Ministry of Reconciliation* found in II Corinthians 5:17-21. What is the result of reconciliation?

3. The Greek word for forgiveness is "aphiemi" and means to let go from one's power, possession, to let go free, escape. (Strong's online concordance) In essence, the intent of Biblical forgiveness is to cut someone loose. In your journal, draw a word picture for forgiving others in which the "unforgi**ven**" is roped to the back of the "unforgiv**ing**."

Unforgiveness is the means by which we securely bind ourselves to that which we hate most. Forgiveness is the practice of cutting loose the person roped to your back. In Psalms 51, David confessed his sin of adultery with Bathsheba, and the murder (blood guilt) of having her husband Uriah killed. David begged God for mercy and asked him to create in him a pure heart. Verse 17 says the sacrifices of God are a broken spirit and a broken and contrite heart. If we are still refusing to accept God's forgiveness for the abortion decision, then we are hanging on to a spirit of pride and self-centeredness. God wants a humble, broken, contrite heart.

I John 1:9

9 If we confess our sins, he is faithful and just and will forgive us our sins and purify us from all unrighteousness.

II Corinthians 5:17-21

17 Therefore, if anyone is in Christ, he is a new creation; the old has gone, the new has come! 18 All this is from God, who reconciled us to himself through Christ and gave us the ministry of reconciliation: 19 that God was reconciling the world to himself in Christ, not counting men's sins against them. And he has committed to us the message of reconciliation. 20 We are therefore Christ's ambassadors, as though God were making his appeal through us. We implore you on Christ's behalf: Be reconciled to God. 21 God made him who had no sin to be sin[a] for us, so that in him we might become the righteousness of God.

4. The two lists below explain the differences between proud and broken (humble, contrite) people. Pick any desires or attitudes from the list that may apply to you and any unforgiveness you may hold in your heart from the abortion experience. The list is taken from a message *The Heart God Revives* by Nancy Leigh DeMoss. (Demoss)

Proud People . . . . .

- ☐ Focus on the failures of others
- ☐ Have a critical, fault-finding spirit; look at everyone else's faults with a microscope, but their own with a telescope; look down on others
- ☐ Are self-righteous; look down on others
- ☐ Have an independent, self-sufficient spirit
- ☐ Have to prove that they are right
- ☐ Claim rights; have a demanding spirit
- ☐ Are self-protective of their time, their rights, and their reputation
- ☐ Desire to be served
- ☐ Desire to be a success
- ☐ Desire self-advancement.
- ☐ Keep others at arms' length
- ☐ Are quick to blame others
- ☐ Are concerned with being respectable, with what others think; work to protect their own image and reputation
- ☐ Want to be sure that no one finds out when they have sinned; instinct is to cover up
- ☐ Have a hard time saying, "I was wrong; will you please forgive me?"
- ☐ Are concerned about the consequences of their sin
- ☐ Wait for the other to come and ask forgiveness when there is a misunderstanding or conflict in relationships
- ☐ Don't think they have anything to repent of

Broken People . . . . .

- ☐ Are overwhelmed with a sense of their own spiritual need
- ☐ Are compassionate; can forgive much because they have been forgiven; esteem all others better than themselves
- ☐ Esteem all others better than themselves
- ☐ Have a dependent spirit; recognize their need for others
- ☐ Are willing to yield the right to be right
- ☐ Yield their rights; have a meek spirit
- ☐ Are self denying
- ☐ Are motivated to serve others
- ☐ Are motivated to be faithful and to make others a success
- ☐ Desire to promote others
- ☐ Are willing to risk getting close to others and to take risks of loving intimately
- ☐ Accept personal responsibility and can see where they are wrong in a situation
- ☐ Are concerned with being real; what matters to them is not what others think but what God knows; are willing to die to their own reputation
- ☐ Once broken, don't care who knows or who finds out; are willing to be exposed because they have nothing to lose
- ☐ Are quick to admit failure and to seek forgiveness when necessary
- ☐ Are grieved over the cause, the root of their sin
- ☐ Take the initiative to be reconciled when there is a misunderstanding or a conflict in relationships; they race to the cross; they see if they can get there first, no matter how wrong the other may have been
- ☐ Realize they have need of a continual heart attitude of repentance

Forgiveness is an act of will, not an emotion. In the Inspirational Study Bible by Max Lucado, he says, "*The first step toward forgiveness is to see the other person as a human being, not as a source of hurt.*" (Lucado, 1995) When God sent his son Jesus to die for our sins, He did just that . . . He saw our human worth. He became one of us, and as a result, when He hung on the cross, He could look at those who were crucifying Him and ask God to forgive them. Max Lucado goes on to say that "*when you forgive someone, you are as close to God as you will ever be, because in that forgiveness you are demonstrating the very heart of God, the merciful King. If you want to understand God, if you want to draw closer to him, then forgive someone today.*"

5. See Pg. 73. Read the parable of the unforgiving servant in Matthew 18:21-35. For what sin (debt) has God forgiven you?

6. Are there "fellow servants" in your life that you can't forgive?

I (Millie) once heard an evangelist state the following: "*you choose to be offended.*" Well, that was hard for me to understand until the Lord finally showed me the ABC's of Behavior (what I call it), which is also known as REBT, Ellis' Rational Emotive Behavioral Therapy. (albertellisinfo.com)

7. Refer to the anger cycle in Chapter 4 and make a note in your journal. See Pg. 73. According to II Corinthians 10:5 we can choose to be offended . . . or choose not to be offended. Remember our feelings are controlled by our thoughts (or belief) about the situation.

8. "Dear God, I choose to forgive _____. I release them from my judgment and place them into your hands of mercy and justice."

9. Look back in Chapter 3, question 13, and for every loss you listed on your **Life Impact Timeline**, release any unforgiveness you may hold in your heart toward the person connected with the offense of the loss. Make a note in your journal.

Sometimes we say we can't forgive because we don't "feel like forgiving," or we will forgive, but we will "never forget." Both of these are only excuses once we have taken forgiveness by the hand on this journey of recovery and looked at this pit stop of healing through God's eyes, His love, mercy, and justice. When we truly forgive ourselves and others . . . it won't hurt anymore when we remember it!

Matthew 18:21-35

[21] Then Peter came to Jesus and asked, "Lord, how many times shall I forgive my brother when he sins against me? Up to seven times?"

[22] Jesus answered, "I tell you, not seven times, but seventy-seven times.[a]

[23] "Therefore, the kingdom of heaven is like a king who wanted to settle accounts with his servants. [24] As he began the settlement, a man who owed him ten thousand talents[b] was brought to him. [25] Since he was not able to pay, the master ordered that he and his wife and his children and all that he had be sold to repay the debt.

[26] "The servant fell on his knees before him. 'Be patient with me,' he begged, 'and I will pay back everything.' [27] The servant's master took pity on him, canceled the debt and let him go.

[28] "But when that servant went out, he found one of his fellow servants who owed him a hundred denarii.[c] He grabbed him and began to choke him. 'Pay back what you owe me!' he demanded.

[29] "His fellow servant fell to his knees and begged him, 'Be patient with me, and I will pay you back.'

[30] "But he refused. Instead, he went off and had the man thrown into prison until he could pay the debt. [31] When the other servants saw what had happened, they were greatly distressed and went and told their master everything that had happened.

[32] "Then the master called the servant in. 'You wicked servant,' he said, 'I canceled all that debt of yours because you begged me to. [33] Shouldn't you have had mercy on your fellow servant just as I had on you?' [34] In anger his master turned him over to the jailers to be tortured, until he should pay back all he owed.

[35] "This is how my heavenly Father will treat each of you unless you forgive your brother from your heart."

II Corinthians 10:5

[5] We demolish arguments and every pretension that sets itself up against the knowledge of God, and we take captive every thought to make it obedient to Christ.

Truth for your Tank

"*Be kind and compassionate to one another, forgiving each other, just as in Christ, God forgave you.*" Ephesians 4:32

Summary Question: Explain the importance of a contrite heart (Psalms 51) when it comes to healing after an abortion experience in the areas of receiving forgiveness from God, forgiving others, and forgiving self.

" *In this sad world of ours, sorrow comes to all . . .
It comes with bitterest agony . . . Perfect relief is not
possible, except with time. You cannot now realize
that you will ever feel better. Is not this so? And
yet it is a mistake. You are sure to be happy again.
To know this, which is certainly true, will make you
some less miserable now. I have had experience
enough to know what I say.*"

~ *Abraham Lincoln*

The Science of Sex
Bonding & Breaking Sexual Soul Ties

According to Genesis 2:24 when a man and woman join together in intimate sexual relations, they become one. Being made in God's image, humans are complex, multi-dimensional beings. We have an intellectual, moral, emotional, physical and social domain. All of these domains together make us a whole person. Our sexuality is woven throughout each of these domains and our sexual decisions affect each one of them, thus affecting our whole person. The brain is our largest sex organ. Everything that happens sexually starts in the brain. The brain releases various chemicals and hormones during sexual arousal and release. These chemicals create a sense of well-being, and make us want to do this activity over again. So, when we open the sexual pathway, a person is more likely to continue on in sexual activity. And, if their relationship breaks up, they're more likely to initiate sex even sooner in the next relationship.

The hormone oxytocin bonds us together in human relationships like super glue. Scientists have known for a long time that mammals who mate for life release oxytocin, and mammals that are promiscuous, do not release oxytocin. (http://www.oxytocin.org/oxytoc/love-science.html) Studies blocking oxytocin release in monogamous mammals caused them to become promiscuous, and injecting oxytocin in the promiscuous mammals caused them to become monogamous. Scientists knew that women release oxytocin during birth and breastfeeding so they began to study the role oxytocin played in bonding human relationships. They found that both men and women release high levels of oxytocin during sexual arousal and release . . . and confirmed that oxytocin is involved in bonding two people together, with the goal of bonding them for life. However in our sexual culture, with people having multiple sexual partners, they've begun to see how oxytocin release is impaired with multiple partners . . . oxytocin release is reduced with each subsequent sexual partner. The bonding works like duct tape. Multiple sexual partners is like trying to reuse the duct tape. After several uses, it doesn't stick anymore. This is due primarily to our bodies releasing endorphins called opiates during emotional pain. The more emotional pain, the more opiates are produced and released. The more opiates released, the less oxytocin is produced and released.

On the next journal page, do the following:
1) Make a list of each previous sexual partner.
2) Confess each sexual sin against God, the person, and against your own body.
3) Repent and ask God's forgiveness, believing He cleanses you from all unrighteousness.
4) Forgive the person for any perpetration against you, or ask them for forgiveness for any victimization from you.
5) Discard all personal items or reminders from the relationship.
6) Ask God to break the soul tie or bond with that partner.
7) Change any old patterns of thinking toward the person. Expose the lies that have been ingrained because of what has happened and find the truth, taking every thought captive according to II Corinthians 10:5.
8) Ask God to restore your purity and practice secondary virginity until marriage.

When finished, it is very freeing to tear the list into small pieces and burn them. Then pour colored red water over the ashes representing the blood of Jesus covering all sins.

My Journey

Chapter Six
Valley of Depression

Everyone comes to crossroads in their life that present several paths of which we can follow. One is led by darkness, which will bring you to a valley of depression along with hopelessness and despair. The other is led by light that desires to bring you to truth, where hope thrives and lifts you up.

It would be so easy if, when faced with life altering choices, we could clearly see the defining differences of the two paths. But unfortunately, we often cannot see, for our vision is impaired due to the negative emotions that cloud our perception of truth; for in the midst of fear . . . lies become our truth.

Emotions run deep when you find yourself faced with an unplanned pregnancy. Your thoughts become scrambled as you consider what path to choose. I (Sherry) remember when I was there. I rationalized my choice of abortion, as I chose to believe it was a blob of tissue and not a child.

When a man or woman chooses abortion or is coerced or forced into one, he/she will soon discover they have walked right into the valley of depression. A sense of constant sadness becomes so heavy that they cannot breathe . . . like a slow death. In Deuteronomy 30:19 God says, "*This day I call heaven and earth as witnesses against you that I have set before you life and death, blessings and curses. Now choose life, so that you and your children may live.*" Abortion not only takes a life of an innocent child but breathes death into the mother and the father. An abortion experience opens the door of death and leads to darkness.

The valley of depression can consume you; however, when we reach upward toward God with a sincere heart, he will take our hand. "*I waited patiently for the Lord, and he turned to me and heard my cry. He lifted me out of the slimy pit, out of the mud and mire; he set my feet on a rock and gave me a firm place to stand.*"
(Psalm 40:1,2)

In order to make a U TURN out of the valley of depression, we must choose the light and begin speaking the truth. (John 3:20,21) The spoken word is more powerful than the unspoken word. (Proverbs 18:21) When you "feel" that you are slipping backwards into the valley of depression (death), cry out and trust God. *"Unless the Lord had given me help, I would soon have dwelt in the silence of death. When I said 'my foot is slipping,' your love, Oh Lord, supported me. When anxiety was great within me, your consolation brought joy to my soul."* (Psalm 94:17-19)

1. How can you relate to the psalmist in Psalm 32:3-5 (see pg. 82) after your abortion? In a few words describe how you felt.

2. See Pg. 82. What does God promise to do?
   Psalm 30:11,12

   Psalm 40:3

   Isaiah 42:16

   Isaiah 61:1-3

3. See Pg. 82. Read Psalm 141:3 and Psalm 19:14. What steps are you going to take to change your words from death to life?

Guilt

Guilt is an emotional experience that occurs when a person realizes or believes he or she has violated a moral standard or law. A man or woman who has chosen abortion will at some point realize that he/she has chosen to kill his or her unborn child instead of following their natural instinct to protect. Remorse will soon follow, caused by the feeling of responsibility for committing this offense. A man or woman will try to ignore the guilt, but it is only a matter of time before it manifests itself in outward behavior. Those who were forced into abortion feel despair and helplessness and often blame themselves for allowing it to happen.

False guilt is based on self-condemning feelings, a superficial (worldly) sorrow that leads to separation from God. (2 Corinthians 7:11) It is also a **false guilt** when you continue to condemn yourself even though you have confessed your sin and asked for God's forgiveness; or if you continue to condemn yourself when it wasn't your fault. (Romans 8:1) This can cause a deep sense of unworthiness.

True guilt will motivate a change and a Godly sorrow or remorse that will help us understand that we have sinned and need forgiveness. "*Godly sorrow brings repentance that leads to salvation and leaves no regrets."* (2 Corinthians 7:10)

Psalm 32:3-5

3 When I kept silent, my bones wasted away through my groaning all day long. 4 For day and night your hand was heavy upon me; my strength was sapped as in the heat of summer. *Selah* 5 Then I acknowledged my sin to you and did not cover up my iniquity. I said, "I will confess my transgressions to the LORD"—and you forgave the guilt of my sin. *Selah*

Psalm 30:11,12

11 You turned my wailing into dancing; you removed my sackcloth and clothed me with joy, 12 that my heart may sing to you and not be silent. O LORD my God, I will give you thanks forever.

Psalm 40:3

3 He put a new song in my mouth, a hymn of praise to our God. Many will see and fear and put their trust in the LORD.

Isaiah 42:16

16 I will lead the blind by ways they have not known, along unfamiliar paths I will guide them; I will turn the darkness into light before them and make the rough places smooth. These are the things I will do; I will not forsake them.

Isaiah 61:1-3

1 The Spirit of the Sovereign LORD is on me, because the LORD has anointed me to preach good news to the poor. He has sent me to bind up the brokenhearted, to proclaim freedom for the captives and release from darkness for the prisoners,[a] 2 to proclaim the year of the LORD's favor and the day of vengeance of our God, to comfort all who mourn, 3 and provide for those who grieve in Zion—to bestow on them a crown of beauty instead of ashes, the oil of gladness instead of mourning, and a garment of praise instead of a spirit of despair. They will be called oaks of righteousness, a planting of the LORD for the display of his splendor.

Psalm 141:3

3 Set a guard over my mouth, O LORD; keep watch over the door of my lips.

Psalm 19:14

14 May the words of my mouth and the meditation of my heart be pleasing in your sight, O LORD, my Rock and my Redeemer.

Psalm 51

[1] Have mercy on me, O God, according to your unfailing love; according to your great compassion blot out my transgressions. [2] Wash away all my iniquity and cleanse me from my sin. [3] For I know my transgressions, and my sin is always before me. [4] Against you, you only, have I sinned and done what is evil in your sight, so that you are proved right when you speak and justified when you judge. [5] Surely I was sinful at birth, sinful from the time my mother conceived me. [6] Surely you desire truth in the inner parts[a]; you teach[b] me wisdom in the inmost place. [7] Cleanse me with hyssop, and I will be clean; wash me, and I will be whiter than snow. [8] Let me hear joy and gladness; let the bones you have crushed rejoice. [9] Hide your face from my sins and blot out all my iniquity. [10] Create in me a pure heart, O God, and renew a steadfast spirit within me. [11] Do not cast me from your presence or take your Holy Spirit from me. [12] Restore to me the joy of your salvation and grant me a willing spirit, to sustain me. [13] Then I will teach transgressors your ways, and sinners will turn back to you. [14] Save me from bloodguilt, O God, the God who saves me, and my tongue will sing of your righteousness. [15] O Lord, open my lips, and my mouth will declare your praise. [16] You do not delight in sacrifice, or I would bring it; you do not take pleasure in burnt offerings. [17] The sacrifices of God are[c] a broken spirit; a broken and contrite heart, O God, you will not despise. [18] In your good pleasure make Zion prosper; build up the walls of Jerusalem. [19] Then there will be righteous sacrifices, whole burnt offerings to delight you; then bulls will be offered on your altar.

Psalm 25:3

3 No one whose hope is in you will ever be put to shame, but they will be put to shame who are treacherous without excuse.

Psalm 34:4,5

4 I sought the LORD, and he answered me; he delivered me from all my fears. 5 Those who look to him are radiant; their faces are never covered with shame.

Isaiah 54:4-8

4 "Do not be afraid; you will not suffer shame. Do not fear disgrace; you will not be humiliated. You will forget the shame of your youth and remember no more the reproach of your widowhood. 5 For your Maker is your husband—the LORD Almighty is his name—the Holy One of Israel is your Redeemer; he is called the God of all the earth. 6 The LORD will call you back as if you were a wife deserted and distressed in spirit—a wife who married young, only to be rejected," says your God. 7 "For a brief moment I abandoned you, but with deep compassion I will bring you back. 8 In a surge of anger I hid my face from you for a moment, but with everlasting kindness I will have compassion on you, "says the LORD your Redeemer.

4. In Psalm 51 we find an example of true guilt in David's prayer. See Pg. 83.
    As you read the Psalm reflect on your own abortion experience. Do you still feel
    guilty for your abortion? If so, why? Have you expressed Godly sorrow for your
    choice of abortion or for those who forced you? If not, why not do it now in your
    own words? Please use the journal pages.

Shame

Many times a woman or man will experience shame following an abortion experience.
Shame is a feeling that you have brought dishonor upon yourself and others when you experienced abortion. The roots of the word shame are thought to derive from an older word
meaning "to cover." When you experience an abortion you want to cover it up which can be
exhausting as you make every effort to protect yourself for fear of rejection.

5. Is there any part of your abortion experience that still causes you to feel
    ashamed? Explain. Is there someone you are ashamed to tell? If so, why?

6. See Pg. 83. Read the following scriptures. What do they say to you
    regarding shame? What promises does God give in his Word about relief from
    shame?

    Psalm 25:3

    Psalm 34:4,5

    Isaiah 54:4-8

    Hebrews 12:2 See Pg. 86.

Anxiety

Anxiety following an abortion will weigh us down and try to keep us from moving forward in
the healing journey. (Luke 21:34) Anxiety may increase around anniversary dates of when
the abortion occurred or when the child would have been born. If anxiety goes unrelieved,
it may turn into anguish which can cause physical or mental pain.

7. In times of anguish Romans 8:26 (see pg. 86) can offer truth and comfort.
    What is that truth and comfort?

8. Tears can be a cleansing for the soul and an outward expression of anguish. What promises does God give in Psalm 126:5 and Revelation 7:17?

9. What does God do with our tears? (Psalm 56:8) See Pg. 86.

Suicide

Unresolved grief can become a heavy load to carry for a man or woman after an abortion. He/She may begin to feel that no one cares! Thoughts such as "*I have no right to live!*" play over and over in the mind as the harsh reality of the trauma becomes too hard to face. They may even feel that they should die as a punishment or have a strong desire to be with their child. They may even go as far as planning their self-inflicted death for they see no other way . . . *but there is!* **SUICIDE IS NEVER THE ANSWER!**

10. Who is our enemy and how can we stop him according to 1 Peter 5:6-9 and Ephesians 6:13-18? See Pg. 86.

11. See Pg. 87. In John 10:10, Satan is compared to a thief. What does he want to do to you? What does the verse say about Jesus?

You are valuable to God! (John 3:16) Your identity as a child of God is based on who Jesus Christ is and what he has done on the cross, NOT what you have done or what has happened in your past. (Psalm 103:10-12)

12. See Pg. 87. Read the following verses. What is God's message to you according to His Word?

Romans 8:1-2

Romans 8:28, 31-39

Philippians 1:6

Hebrews 4:16

Hebrews 12:2

2 Let us fix our eyes on Jesus, the author and perfecter of our faith, who for the joy set before him endured the cross, scorning its shame, and sat down at the right hand of the throne of God.

Romans 8:26

26 In the same way, the Spirit helps us in our weakness. We do not know what we ought to pray for, but the Spirit himself intercedes for us with groans that words cannot express.

Psalm 126:5

5 Those who sow in tears will reap with songs of joy.

Revelation 7:17

17 For the Lamb at the center of the throne will be their shepherd; he will lead them to springs of living water. And God will wipe away every tear from their eyes."

Psalm 56:8 (KJV)

8 Thou tellest my wanderings: put thou my tears into thy bottle: are they not in thy book?

I Peter 5:6-9

6 Humble yourselves, therefore, under God's mighty hand, that he may lift you up in due time. 7 Cast all your anxiety on him because he cares for you. 8 Be self-controlled and alert. Your enemy the devil prowls around like a roaring lion looking for someone to devour. 9 Resist him, standing firm in the faith, because you know that your brothers throughout the world are undergoing the same kind of sufferings.

Ephesians 6:13-18

13 Therefore put on the full armor of God, so that when the day of evil comes, you may be able to stand your ground, and after you have done everything, to stand. 14 Stand firm then, with the belt of truth buckled around your waist, with the breastplate of righteousness in place, 15 and with your feet fitted with the readiness that comes from the gospel of peace. 16 In addition to all this, take up the shield of faith, with which you can extinguish all the flaming arrows of the evil one. 17 Take the helmet of salvation and the sword of the Spirit, which is the word of God. 18 And pray in the Spirit on all occasions with all kinds of prayers and requests. With this in mind, be alert and always keep on praying for all the saints.

John 10:10

[10] The thief comes only to steal and kill and destroy; I have come that they may have life, and have it to the full.

Romans 8:1-2

[8] Therefore, there is now no condemnation for those who are in Christ Jesus,[a] [2] because through Christ Jesus the law of the Spirit of life set me free from the law of sin and death.

Romans 8:28, 31-39

[28] And we know that in all things God works for the good of those who love him,[a] who[b] have been called according to his purpose.

[31] What, then, shall we say in response to this? If God is for us, who can be against us? [32] He who did not spare his own Son, but gave him up for us all—how will he not also, along with him, graciously give us all things? [33] Who will bring any charge against those whom God has chosen? It is God who justifies. [34] Who is he that condemns? Christ Jesus, who died —more than that, who was raised to life — at the right hand of God and is also interceding for us. [35] Who shall separate us from the love of Christ? Shall trouble or hardship or persecution or famine or nakedness or danger or sword? [36] As it is written:

"For your sake we face death all day long; we are considered as sheep to be slaughtered."[a]

[37] No, in all these things we are more than conquerors through him who loved us. [38] For I am convinced that neither death nor life, neither angels nor demons,[b] neither the present nor the future, nor any powers, [39] neither height nor depth, nor anything else in all creation, will be able to separate us from the love of God that is in Christ Jesus our Lord.

Phillipians 1:6

[6] being confident of this, that he who began a good work in you will carry it on to completion until the day of Christ Jesus.

Hebrews 4:16

[16] Let us then approach the throne of grace with confidence, so that we may receive mercy and find grace to help us in our time of need.

Truth for your Tank

"Forget the former things; do not dwell on the past. See, I am doing a new thing! Now it springs up; do you not perceive it? I am making a way in the desert and streams in the wasteland." Isaiah 43:18,19

Summary Question: One new way that I have learned to help keep myself out of the valley of depression is . . .

What steps can I take to make my life better?

My Journey

The Legend of the Tear Jar
Pleasant White, Ph.D.

In the dry climate of ancient Greece, water was prized above all. Giving up water from one's own body, when crying tears for the dead, was considered a sacrifice. They caught their precious tears in tiny pitchers or "tear jars" like the one shown here (life sized.) The tears became holy water and could be used to sprinkle on doorways to keep out evil or to cool the brow of a sick child.

The tear jars were kept unpainted until the owner had experienced the death of a parent, sibling, child or spouse. After that, the grieving person decorated the tear jar with intricate designs, and examples of these can still be seen throughout modern Greece.

This ancient custom symbolizes the transformation that takes place in people who have grieved deeply. They are not threatened by the grief of people in pain. They have been in the depths of pain themselves, and returned. Like the tear jar, they can now be with others who grieve and catch their tears.
(Pleasant White)

Note: The average human body contains 10 gallons of water. Early Christians were buried with bottles of their tears because they knew God valued them. Remember Psalm 56:8.

Expressing what you're feeling is the first

step to healing !

~ Millie Lace, MSE, LPC

Chapter Seven

Carried by God's Grace

I remember picking up a paper years ago titled, *WHO AM I* (in Christ).

I (Millie) have used the truths presented in that paper in my professional counseling office for years. Why? At least 90% of my clients have been those struggling with their self-worth. No, that wasn't their presenting problem, for they may have presented with relationship problems, addiction problems, grief, etc. Yet, sometime during the journey of the sessions, I would sense the need to introduce these concepts. Many times I have had clients begin to cry as they would hear lines like . . . *"I Am my beloved's; I Am chosen; I Am a new creation; I Am reconciled to God; I Am a saint; I Am a joint heir with Christ; I Am righteous and holy; I Am justified; I Am bought with a price; I Am redeemed and forgiven; I Am a partaker of His divine nature; I Am complete in Christ; I Am a recipient of His lavish grace."* God carries us with His grace.

Ephesians 2:8,9 says, *"For it is by grace you have been saved through faith and this not from yourselves lest any man should boast, it is the gift of God, not by works so that no one can boast."* I cannot be good enough or buy it . . . for grace is a gift! It is only because I am carried by His grace that I am able to write this study chapter. The reality of the trauma and the sin of abortion is too heavy . . . I finally laid it all down at the cross. The precious blood of Christ and His death, burial and resurrection has conquered sin and freed me from my past. After admitting the sin of elective or coerced abortion and asking for God's forgiveness, it only takes the surrendering of my will to yield to the spirit of God who loves me and desires to lavish His grace upon me. He is waiting with outstretched hands to carry you too. Will you let Him?

Living in grace is a learned behavior. And God is more concerned about your living out your full potential, the person you should have been, than you are concerned about it! Remember the cat looking in the mirror at the end of Chapter 2?

God had a plan, and abortion was not part of it; but He allowed it to happen, because He gives us free will. God permits what He hates to accomplish what He loves. So if we approach God with a contrite heart and spirit, He wants to restore us and allow us to be a partaker of His DIVINE NATURE! (II Peter 1:4) Oh my! What love! Ephesians 2:10 says, "*For we are God's workmanship, created in Christ Jesus to do good works, which God prepared in advance for us to do.*" So, His grace is bigger than sin. **We need to wake up by Grace!** How do we stay in the river of grace without our thoughts and feelings about the abortion experience overwhelming us? Spiritual growth is handcrafted, not mass produced.

1. See Pg. 94. Read John 7:37,38. What must you do to have the streams of living water flowing from you?

2. *Love Lifted Me* is a song written in 1911 by Howard E. Smith. The chorus line reads, "*Love lifted Me, Love lifted Me, when nothing else could help, love lifted me.*" (Smith) Do you feel that love has lifted you from the valley of depression surrounding the abortion experience to a place of His forgiving mercy and grace? If not, pray, examine your conscience, and ask God to let you see what is in your heart that is keeping you in doubt or blocking your faith. Write your thoughts and prayers here.

3. Do you feel carried by God's grace? It is very normal to not "*feel*" forgiven. But remember, forgiveness is not based on our feelings but on God's truth of His love for us. If you do feel carried by God's grace, forgiven for or forgiving of the sin of abortion, and restored to a right relationship with God, then write a "convincing, persuasive speech" to the group on your journal page to assure them and yourself of this truth.

John 7:37,38

[37] On the last and greatest day of the Feast, Jesus stood and said in a loud voice, "If anyone is thirsty, let him come to me and drink. [38] Whoever believes in me, as[a] the Scripture has said, streams of living water will flow from within him."

Ephesians 2: 4-7

[4] But because of his great love for us, God, who is rich in mercy, [5] made us alive with Christ even when we were dead in transgressions —it is by grace you have been saved. [6] And God raised us up with Christ and seated us with him in the heavenly realms in Christ Jesus, [7] in order that in the coming ages he might show the incomparable riches of his grace, expressed in his kindness to us in Christ Jesus.

In Acts 8 and 9, Saul was among those who were stoning Christians like Stephen. Chapter 8 says Saul was destroying the church. In Chapter 9 the Bible says he was "*breathing out murderous threats against the Lord's disciples.*" He would go to the high priest and ask for letters to the synagogues in Damascus, so that if he found any there who belonged to the Way (the early Christian church), whether men or women, he was planning on taking them as prisoners to Jerusalem. But the world's worst murder becomes God's greatest salvation. Abortion is murder and yet God wants to redeem that sin and transform us to a new creature. He wants to make us His evangelists to tell others of this saving grace that carries us. For Saul became the apostle Paul. Again, God permits what He hates to accomplish what He loves. And Lamentations 3:22,23 says, "*Because of the Lord's great love, we are not consumed, for His compassions never fail. They are new every morning.*"

So what does it mean to feel loved by God? John Piper, Christian author described it this way while speaking at the American Association of Christian Counselor's Conference, "*Feeling loved by God is that He is crushing every desire that competes with Him.*" (Piper, 2009) He loves us because He created us for His pleasure. Imagine a falling rock and a spider web trying to stop it. Our weight of sin is like the falling rock . . . nothing can stop us except the mere pleasure and power of God. He carries us in his hand. He is sovereign! So what is the love of God for you? His relentless pursuit of your praise. He labors to display himself to us—to show, prove, or manifest the immeasurableness of His grace.

4. See Pg. 95. Read Ephesians 2:4-7 and meditate on God's love for you. Shut your eyes and imagine that you are standing under a beautiful waterfall. Allow yourself to feel God's love washing over you as the water falls on your head over your entire body.

5. 1 John 3:1 says, "*See what great love the Father has **lavished** on us, that we should be called children of God!*" What comes to mind when you think of the word lavished?

6. Ephesians 2:10 says, "*For we are God's workmanship, created in Christ Jesus to do good works, which God prepared in advance {His plan} for us to do.*" God longs for us to come back to Him, even after our abortion experience. Why?

John 1:14 says,"*The Word became flesh and made his dwelling among us. We have seen his glory, the glory of the One and Only, who came from the Father, full of grace and truth.*" And verse 16, "*From the fullness of grace we have all received one blessing after another.*" Or, we have received grace upon grace! This powerful, transforming, life changing, divine grace comes to us from Christ's fullness through seeing the glory of the Son of God, or the light beam that shines from Him into our hearts. "*And we, with unveiled faces all reflect the Lord's glory, are being transformed into his likeness with ever-increasing glory, which comes from the Lord, who is the Spirit.*" (II Corinthians 3:18) When Jesus died on the cross, the veil in the temple was rent or torn in two . . . torn for me and for you. We have a piece of the veil! We can come boldly to the throne for we are joint heirs with Christ.

God loves us and adopted us as His sons (and daughters) in accordance with His pleasure and will to the praise of his glorious grace. God doesn't love us just to affirm our desire to be loved or to be made much of, because this is the natural way to love, and it wouldn't require anything supernatural. It is natural to give affirmation to someone we love.

But we exist to praise the glory of God! **So God carries us by His grace for His glory! He desires the praise!** (Ephesians 1:1-14) Praising the glory of the grace of God is the all satisfying goal of life, the apex of this journey, not how we get there. Being reconciled, redeemed, and restored to a "wholeness" in Christ is only possible from seeing God's glory that gives rise to the praise. He promises to keep changing us from glory to glory as we are transformed to His image. Christ laid down His life to display the glory of God's grace and to captivate or charm us with Himself. When we finally see God's love this way, experience this miracle in our lives, then our fascination with ourselves will be humbled or contrite before God, and we will behold His glory!

> "*With humility and confidence, open your hearts to repentance. Your merciful Father awaits you, so he can give you His pardon and peace.*"
>
> ~ John Paul II to those who have had abortions . . . *The Gospel of Life,* 99

97

Truth for your Tank

"*From the fullness of His grace we have all received one blessing after another.*"
John 1:16

Summary Question: Explain what "carried by grace" means to you.

My Journey

Chapter Eight
Letting Go

First thing, I (Pauly) want you to raise your right hand high in the air, now bend at the elbow toward your back, now pat yourself . . . you deserve it after all the hard work I know you have done up to this point in this study.

Many men and women have blazed this trail before you, and often times this part in our journey can be a scary one. It is time to recognize, accept, and then let go of our babies. Not letting go in the sense that we don't know what is happening to them, but letting them go into our Heavenly Father's hands, where they will be safe for all eternity. I have finally realized that letting go is to fear less and to love more. To let go doesn't mean to stop caring; it means I can't do it for someone else. To let go is not to deny but to accept. To let go is not to cut myself off; it's the realization that I can't control another. To let go is not to judge, but to allow another to be a human being. To let go is to admit powerlessness, which means the outcome is not in my hands. To let go is not to try to change or blame another; I can only change myself. To let go is not to adjust everything to my desires, but to take each day as it comes, relax and to cherish the moment.

In my own healing journey I did not acknowledge my baby as a person until I was in my recovery program. For the first time, I said his name, Owen. Just saying it brought comfort to my heart. Saying his name gave identity and honor to him. **Letting go of our babies is not a onetime event but a process.** For me, I grieved for about a year after the ending of the study. It was different than the emotions I felt before. It wasn't anger, depression, or unforgiveness, but just a genuine recognition of my loss. I had days where I felt sad, days that I missed him, and I realized that it was ok to feel that way.   Losing the physical presence of our babies to abortion is a loss just as losing the physical presence of a parent to cancer, or a friend in a car wreck. But the connection to that child is unique and so is the loss.

Grieving the death of your child involves a connection like no other. While doing research recently, I (Millie) have learned that scientists from the American Academy of Pediatrics now recognize that cells traffic between fetus and mother during pregnancy.

The name of the process is called *Fetal Microchimerism* (FMC) and has been "*demonstrated to persist for years, probably for a lifetime in the circulation of normal women.*" Fetal cells pass into the maternal circulation during normal human pregnancy. Evidence of fetal cells in the mother's circulation has been described as early as 4-5 weeks of gestation. (Anne Stevens, 2002) Talk about a bond . . . a connection like no other! No wonder the evidence of the loss is inside us, not just emotionally, but literally . . . physically inside of us!!

Death has touched our lives and we need to mourn that loss—not only the mothers, but fathers, family members, anyone who has been affected by the abortion experience. My husband Dail has shared many times of how much he misses not being able to celebrate his daughter's first birthday, her first day of school, or walking her down the homecoming court.

Attending a funeral for a loved one does not mean when you leave there you will not feel sad or miss them. But attending the funeral does help to bring closure to the loss of their physical presence on this earth. **This is what a memorial service is for—to help you publicly acknowledge your child by name, give them honor by celebrating the sanctity of their life in a special way, and then to release your child to God.** He promises in Matthew 5:4, "*Blessed are those who mourn, for they will be comforted.*" Also in II Corinthians 5:6-8, the Bible says that when we are absent in body we are home with the Lord.

One of my favorite scriptures is Hebrews 11:1, "*Now faith is being sure of what we hope for and certain of what we do not see.*" When I (Millie) was growing up I always knew I had a sister in heaven. She would have been born before me, but she died right before her birth because of hydrocephalus. My mom would often say her name, Virginia Ann.

Years later when my mom was dying of cancer, we would talk about heaven and what it would be like—streets of gold, and yes . . . mom would see Virginia Ann! Then right after my mom died, one night I was sad and crying because of missing her physical presence. Oh, I longed to see her. My mom was my best friend! Then, all of a sudden, I felt as if I was being whisked up and away into the spirit world . . . and there was my mom—she wasn't sick, but young and beautiful! And she was carrying her baby, Virginia Ann, who was so chubby, healthy and adorable! I kept reaching out to them but my mom and her baby went on through what looked like a curtain in front of a stage, and I could not reach them or see them anymore. And just about the time I knew I couldn't go any further, I saw sparks of light all gathered in a huge area.

As I looked closer, I could see them . . . millions of babies all wanting me to pick them up! Then as soon as it had happened it was over, and I was back in my real world. Wow, what had happened? I began to ask God to help me understand the meaning. Knowing that my husband Dail and I have a daughter who we chose to abort in 1979, I wondered if this was assurance for us that yes, someday we will hold her in heaven.

Then, it seems as if the Holy Spirit whispered that not only would we someday pick up our daughter, but also all of the other parents who have had children die from abortion would pick up their children too. God wants all the parents of aborted babies to come to know Him so they can have the wonderful joy of reuniting with their children in heaven. After all, as artist Lynne Marie Davis has demonstrated in her lesson *Jesus Delivers*, our child's spirit has been with Jesus since He delivered them on the abortion table! (Davis, 2009) And Hebrews 12:1 says that we are surrounded by a "*great cloud of witnesses.*"

So, faith is being certain of what we do not see. Although we have never seen our aborted babies, God can allow us to know if they are a boy or a girl. I invite you to take time now to pray and ask God to reveal to you, if he hasn't already, who your baby is, the gender and the name. My husband and I named our baby girl Jill Allison.

In the space below, write what the Lord shows you about your child. Give yourself permission to cry, think, feel, imagine what they would look like, and dream what they could have become. Say hello, and write the things you will say when you meet them in heaven. Then ask the Lord to reveal to you the way you and your family might memorialize him or her to say goodbye and release them to His care. Some plant a tree, some buy a teddy bear and dress them either as a girl or boy, and some write a poem or letter. You can do as little or as much as you need. You may find that you choose one way now, and then in six months you may want to do something else. That is okay, it is your grief, and the Lord will lead you through the journey.

One thing I really want to say when I see my baby in heaven is . . .

Truth for your Tank
"*There will be no more night. They will not need the light of a lamp or the light of the sun, for the Lord God will give them light. And they will reign forever and ever.*" Revelation 22:5

Summary Question: I would like to give my child identity and honor, and memorialize them by . . .

Baby Names

There are thousands of baby names. (Names)   Although you may already have one in mind to name your child, here are a few others to choose from:

Anna—mother

Abigail—joy of the Father

Allison—noble, exalted

Bethany—town in Bethlehem

Crystal—jewel

Christiana—follower of Christ

Emma—whole, complete

Faith—sure reliance

Grace—God's favor

Gloria—the glorious

Hannah—good

Kayla—keeper of the keys

Jessica—rich, God beholds

Jill—youthful

Naomi—pleasant, sweet

Olivia—bringer of peace

Pauline—humble

Priscilla—dutiful, lovely

Rebecca—peacemaker

Samantha—listen, name of God

Sarah—princess

Shaina—beautiful

Sophia—wisdom

Zoe—flight, freedom

Alison—noble, exalted

Andrew—manly, brave

Angel—angel

Benjamin—right-hand son

Caleb—like the heart

Daniel—Hebrew name

Eric—princely

Fredrick—peaceful ruler

Jacob—supplanter

Jared—rose, descending

Jason—healer

John—God is gracious

Joseph—may Jehovah add

Hezekiah—God is my strength

Harrison—noble, princely

Kenneth—handsome

Isaiah—God is my helper

Luke—native of Lucania

Matthew—gift of the Lord

Peter—dependable, rock

Samuel—asked of God

Stephen—crown, loyal

Victor—conquering

Zachary—Jehovah hath remembered

My Journey

> " *Abortion affects as many lives as a single life could.* "
>
> ~ Millie Lace, MSE, LPC

Jesus Delivers
Abortion Recovery Art Workshop by Lynne Marie Davis

MATERIALS:

11 x 14 Canvas Board
1" Painter's Tape
1" Flat Brush
#6 or #8 Round White Brush
#2 Pencil
Brown Sharpie Fine Point pen
Round Styrofoam Dinner Plates for Palettes
Water Bowls
Paper Towels for blotting paintbrush
Xerox copy of Left hand and Right hand (see pgs. 110, 112)
2 Sheets 8.5 x 11 Tracing Paper
Acrylic BASICS Paint 4 oz. tubes in the following suggested colors:
    Flesh tone (for white hands)
    Burnt Umber (for black/brown hands)
    Burnt Umber (for earth color)
    White
    Yellow Oxide
    Cadmium Yellow Light
    Brilliant Purple
    Deep Violet
    Pink or Rose
    Light Blue
    Cerulean Blue Hue

DAY 1 or FIRST SESSION - about 30 min.

1. Tape off a border with your painter's tape. You will basically be masking your outside edges.
2. Trace the hands onto your tracing paper with your #2 pencil.
3. Rub the pencil onto the back of the traced hand images.
4. Place the hands right side up in position on your canvas and trace onto the canvas.
5. Outline the hands with your brown permanent marker.

You will be ready to begin your workshop.

Jesus Delivers
Abortion Recovery Art Workshop by Lynne Marie Davis

Introduction

The original painting was done from a vision given to the sibling of a post-abortive woman who was tormented by the sight/sounds of an abortion.

"It was a day or so after I had spoken with my sister on the phone. Nothing directly was said about the abortion—more about other physical and emotional trials that she was dealing with and trying to overcome. I did not know if she was making a connection between the past and the present, but I knew that there was one.

"This time, as I was reflecting on our conversation and allowing the usual traumatic images to run through my mind, the Lord suddenly broke through with these words firmly spoken, '*That Never Happened.*' That alone caused me to stop short . . . but then He replaced those old images with a vision.

"A flood of understanding without words poured over me. I 'looked' at what He was showing me. As I looked, I realized He was saying that everything that we had regarded as fact about that day - were not His facts. He was saying, 'That Never Happened. Look, this is what happened.'

"In the vision I was as a woman about to give birth. I saw the Lord's nail-pierced hands reaching forward to receive my baby. Then this is what was communicated to my spirit:

'I was in the room before you got there. I knew this day was coming and I was waiting for you. I took the baby. I delivered your baby. I received your baby and the earthsuit was returned to the earth. See my nail scarred hands? At that very moment, where sin abounded, My Grace did much more abound. I am the Lord and I took the baby. I won the victory. I always win.

My hands are still open. Open for you. Do not doubt. Your family is united in my heart through my blood and soon we all will be united face to face.'"

Jesus Delivers
Abortion Recovery Art Workshop by Lynne Marie Davis

DAY 2 - Art Workshop
You will need to have each participant's place set with:
Paint Brushes
Bowl of Water
2 Paper Plate Palettes (about a quarter size amount of paint on each)
   Brown, Purple and Blue colors on one plate
   White, Yellow and Pink colors on the other plate
Paper Towel folded next to canvas to blot off extra paint

BEGIN: (Quotation marks indicate what the leader says while directing participants in the art workshop.)
"Jesus" (or you might say "Father, Son and Holy Spirit"), "Who knows the end from the beginning, was already on the scene."

ROUND BRUSH SECTION:
"Paint the hands first. Think of Him as receiving you this very moment. His hands are extended as an invitation to come and join Him and consider His version of what took place . . . '*Come let us reason together . . .*' They are welcoming hands. They reach for you in longing for fellowship.

"Then paint the holes in His hands or wrist. Be mindful that the sin was paid for on that day on Calvary. Even as He was pierced, His thoughts were specifically on you and your baby. "Consider the price of Love."

FLAT BRUSH SECTION:
"Next go to the bottom of your canvas and choose your brown paint representing the earth, the world.

"Add your brown to the bottom of the canvas using your 1" flat brush. We are reminding ourselves that our 'forms' are of the earth, but our LIFE was breathed into us by our Father.

"Now you can take any combination of paint and begin to paint your purples, pinks, gold, and white up through the redeeming hands of Jesus. You are cooperating with Him in reenacting what really took place at that moment. Moving the baby, sending the baby, paint up and through experiencing the flow of the baby's spirit/soul being received into the hands of Jesus—just as He said took place. Leaving the brown paint, the earthy, the earthsuit behind. We are focusing on His Truth now—remembering that Grace at that moment was MUCH MORE abounding—paint up, paint up through His hands the soul and spirit.

"After you have delivered your baby into the hands of Jesus, just indicate by color (pink for girl, blue for boy) and a few round shapes where your baby is now resting. As you do this, God will begin to show you the reality of it. Let Him speak to you, minister to you.

"Lastly—you can paint the Glory of Heaven—adding jewels, stones, the baby name in glitter letters, etc. As you finish your piece and stand back to look at it—notice the hands of Jesus still open toward you. Not in the distance somewhere—not out there somewhere but in your Now and in your Today. Today is always the Day of Salvation—and **It** is TODAY! **Amen!**"

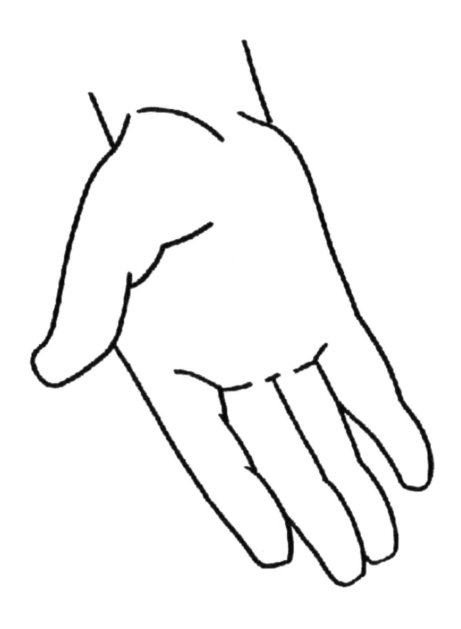

Right Hand Pattern (place hand on left side of canvas when facing board) *Jesus Delivers* Art Workshop
Artist: Lynne Marie Davis,
www.lynnemariedavis.com
Concepts of Truth International, ©2011

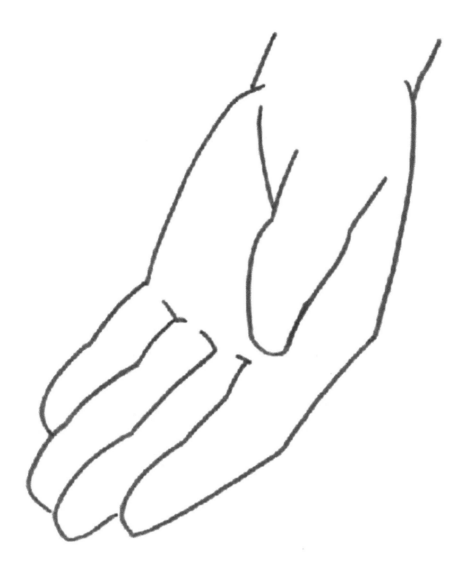

Left Hand Pattern (place hand on right side of canvas when facing board) *Jesus Delivers* Art Workshop
Artist: Lynne Marie Davis,
www.lynnemariedavis.com
Concepts of Truth International, ©2011

Chapter Nine
Continuing the Journey

In 1979 I (Millie) made a mistake and took a doctor's advice to have a D&C to end a 7-week pregnancy. My husband Dail and I will always have regret that we took the life of our daughter, Jill Allison. We lived in denial for over 12 years wearing our masks, justifying, rationalizing, and trying to live Christian lives; yet the problem would not go away. We finally heard someone give testimony to God's grace, love and forgiveness and that gave us courage to begin to take off our masks and deal with it. We had to acknowledge the sin, ask forgiveness, work through the anger, forgive others, accept God's forgiveness (forgive ourselves), mourn and memorialize our baby girl—**the exact steps that you have completed in this journey.**

But remember it was the **testimony** to God's grace that encouraged us to seek help. It will be **your testimony** that serves as tangible proof or evidence of your freedom from the haunting past of abortion. Testimony comes from the word "test-a-ment" which means tangible proof. "Test-a-ment" comes from the Latin word "testari" which means to be a witness. Jesus is a "test-a-ment" or a sacrament of the covenant that God made with man because Jesus came to earth in human form. (Merriam-Webster Online Dictionary) He "Testified" for God! When we have the spirit of God living in us through Jesus Christ, we too are a testament for God. Our very lives are a testimony, a holy sacrament, a tangible proof of grace and truth!

John 1:14 says, "*The **Word** became **flesh** and made his dwelling among us. We have **seen** his glory, the glory of the one and only Son, who came from the Father, full of grace and truth.*"

"***Shame is the ultimate silencer.***" I have used that quote for years because it was so profound in my life. As long as I was silent in my shame from the abortion, the enemy of my soul kept me from fulfilling the plan that God had intended. God has a purpose in our pain. Romans 8:28 says, "*And we know that in all things God works for the good of those who love him, who have been called according to his purpose.*" So, in continuing this journey, you will have moments that you may feel the shame trying to creep back in. In those times you must remember, guilt is necessary for us to admit the sin of an elective or coerced abortion, and you have already done that! Guilt simply says, "I **made** a mistake." If you were forced into an abortion, it was not your fault. However, shame is false guilt and is condemnation. Shame says, "I **am** a mistake!" So, if and when that happens, you will want to refute the lies and give the ol' devil a black eye! How? By testifying to the glory of God's grace in your life!

114

For some, the end of this study is a celebration of the end of their unrest and suffering and the beginning of learning new ways of responding to guilt and sorrow of the past. Praise our Lord Jesus for the healing restoration in our lives! For others, it is not only healing and learning new ways to respond to the past, but also the beginning of another part of the journey that you will continue in a very special unique ministry in which God is calling you.

We strongly believe that a man or woman who has just recently finished this study should not be rushed into sharing his or her experience publicly, prematurely, or too often. A man or woman who has experienced healing should be able to share their story when they feel it is appropriate, but not compulsively. We encourage him or her to hold back, slow down, take time, pray, and count the cost. Then when they are ready, we support and encourage them in every way we can.

Our testimonies are powerful! God will use you in His timing and for His glory to share your testimony in love, giving others permission to come forward—whether it is on a one-to-one individual basis or sharing in a large group at the United Nations! Thus, the ripple effect or the multiplication effect of the early church! We believe after one experiences the grace, mercy, love, and forgiveness after abortion, he or she will want to share with others. Whether privately or publicly, they will want to testify to what God has done! *"They overcame him by the blood of the Lamb and by the word of their testimony . . ."* (Revelation 12:11)

Are you called? Micah 6:8 says, *"He has showed you, O man, what is good. And what does the Lord require of you? To act justly and to love mercy and to walk humbly with your God."* So, no matter what . . . act justly, love mercy and walk humbly with God. He will lead you in His timing. But the key is to listen and obey.

We named this chapter **Continuing the Journey** because we will all be healing from now until eternity, until we meet Jesus and our babies face to face. Yes, we **can** heal to a place to help others, a place without penitence, a place without the shame attached, a place where we will share with so much passion that others will join us, start their journey, and help others heal too! That, my friend, **is** the ultimate continuation of this journey. So take heart and be encouraged!

1. See Pg. 116. Read Romans 15:13, and write a prayer for yourself and others.

2. See Pg. 116. In John 15:9-12, Jesus explains how we continue in this journey. Based on His advice, what can you do to remain in this love? What will be the result?

Romans 15:13

13 May the God of hope fill you with all joy and peace as you trust in him, so that you may overflow with hope by the power of the Holy Spirit.

John 15:9-12

9 "As the Father has loved me, so have I loved you. Now remain in my love. 10 If you obey my commands, you will remain in my love, just as I have obeyed my Father's commands and remain in his love. 11 I have told you this so that my joy may be in you and that your joy may be complete. 12 My command is this: Love each other as I have loved you.

3. When you do feel that you might be ready to share the secret of the abortion experience with someone, ask yourself the following:

   a) What is my motivation for sharing my testimony? *to be honest maybe help someone*

   b) Why do I want to tell this person, and what do I hope to accomplish?

   c) Can I accomplish it? *being honest*

   d) Am I prepared for a different outcome than the one I hope for? *yes*

   e) Will I be able to accept a different outcome? *yes*

After answering the above, pray and ask God's permission and direction. Prepare a quiet and calm time for the meeting. Prepare the person beforehand by saying something like, "*I have something important to talk with you about.*"

You may also want to suggest how you would like for them to respond. "*I'm going to share something very personal with you because I trust you and feel that our relationship will be better when you know this about me. I ask that you remember that this is very hard for me to talk about. If you are angry or upset by what I tell you, I ask that you think before you respond. I hope that when I am through, you will reassure me of your love for me.*"

When telling young children and, only if they ask, give them age appropriate responses with only relevant details. A good example of an appropriate response for children ages 8-10 might be, "*Yes, mommy had a baby growing in her tummy who died before he/she could be born.*"

I remember one of our volunteers praying about when to tell her teenage son. She prayed and not only did God prepare her, but God prepared him! She trusted God, and He orchestrated the event. Telling her teen helped her, and helped her teen make sense out of his life too. Also, if your parents were not involved in the abortion decision, it helps them to understand what happened.

The following is a loving example of telling a mom who is not repentant about her part in her daughter's abortion: "*Mom, I've been doing a Bible study to help me come to peace with God about my abortion. One thing I've realized is that I need to ask you to forgive me for choosing to be sexually active and putting you in the position of having to make that choice for me to have an abortion. Will you please forgive me?*"

An example of what not to say to the unrepentant mom would be, "*You know that abortion you made me have when I was 15? Well, I forgive you.*" Remember in Chapter 1 we said that everyone's story is different but all have common threads? Well, so will each situation of sharing be unique to that individual's circumstances.

4.   List below any individuals who come to your mind that you may want to someday share with about the abortion experience and your healing journey.

So, the time has come when you need to make a plan; for those without a plan, plan to fail. In the counseling process, a plan is the guide to help move us along to our goal. We started on this journey asking, "*Where Am I ?*" We followed the "*Map Maker*" and left our traveling companions of "*Relief & Denial*" behind. We have worked through the anger, guilt, and depression, and we have taken forgiveness by the hand. We have experienced the freedom of being carried by God's grace and letting go of our hold on our "stuff" that would weight us down along the road. So now, we continue the journey and God will be faithful. He will complete the good work that He has begun in you—He promised! "*Being confident of this, that he who began a good work in you will carry it on to completion until the day of Christ Jesus.*" (Philippians 1:6)

Also in your plan, you will need to make every effort (II Peter 1:5) to work in lots of daily meditation, Bible reading, prayer, and rest! But remember, we have a heavenly host praying for us! And, because Jesus **is** the only God-man, He is the **only** mediator between man and God. (1Timothy 2:5) But this in no way means we cannot or should not ask our fellow Christians to pray with us and for us (1 Timothy 2:1-4), including those Christians in heaven who have already had their sanctification completed. For James 5:16 says, ". . . *the prayer of a righteous man is powerful and effective.*" Origen, one of the early church fathers said it this way, "*But not the high priest [Christ] alone prays for those who pray sincerely, but also the angels . . . as also the souls of the saints who have already fallen asleep.*" (Prayer 11 [A.D. 233]) (Origen of Alexandria) So take courage and take hope. Our babies are for us! They are in the heavenly grandstands rallying us on as we continue this journey. Matthew 18:10 says, "*See that you do not despise one of these little ones. For I tell you that their angels in heaven always see the face of my Father in heaven.*"

On a final note, once you have completed a recovery program and the requirements for *Concepts of Recovery The Journey* facilitator training, you have the opportunity to use your gifts for ministry in the abortion recovery mission field. We are a big community of sisters and brothers with the Father, Son, and Holy Spirit leading the journey. We have a great bond between us. We understand and love each other. I know that every area of this ministry could be enhanced by your service. You could empathize with a man or woman in an unplanned pregnancy situation because you have been there. You could challenge teens and single adults to live with sexual health and integrity. You could sit with those who mourn over abortions in their past because you, too, have mourned.

The things in our lives we have been most embarrassed about or ashamed of are the very things God wants to expose and use for His GLORY!
II Corinthians 1:3,4 says, "*Praise be to the God and Father of our Lord Jesus Christ, the Father of compassion and the God of all comfort, who comforts us in all our troubles, so that we can comfort those in any trouble with the comfort we ourselves receive from God.*" Only you and God can decide if you are called to the abortion recovery mission field.

Please call us or email and let us know how God is leading you. Also, we would appreciate if you would fill out the *Future Involvement* checklist on pg. 123 in the back of this book. I want to encourage you to visit our website at internationalhelpline.org for a variety of resources and helpful information. Someone on our staff is available 24/7. You can always call toll free, 866.482.LIFE. Remember, there is grace and peace after abortion!

Continuing the Journey,
Millie Lace, MSE, LPC
Founder/Director
Concepts of Truth International
870.238.4329
Email: info@conceptsoftruth.org

Truth for your Tank

"*May the God of hope fill you with all joy and peace as you trust in him, so that you may overflow with hope by the power of the Holy Spirit.*" Romans 15:13

Summary Question: Write your plan for continuing the journey.

My Journey

" *Life shouldn't be a journey to the grave with the intention of arriving safely in a pretty and well—preserved body, but rather, to skid in broadside, thoroughly used up, totally worn out, and loudly shouting . . .*

'Wow ! What a ride ! Thank You, Lord !' "

~ Beth Moore

Future Involvement

In an effort to keep you informed and "in-touch" with us, please consider participating in these vital support areas:

- o Being on the mailing list
- o Acting as a prayer partner
- o Joining in the Sanctity Of Human Life Annual Memorial Service

The Lord brought us together for a special time, and we have seen Him accomplish wonderful things. Please prayerfully consider what God's next steps will be for you.

(Please check any areas of interest)

- o Concepts of Truth volunteer; i.e., local counselor, administrative help
- o The International Helpline for Abortion Recovery and Prevention Phone Part-Time Staff
- o *Concepts of Recovery The Journey* Group Facilitator/Co-Facilitator
- o Special Events (activities giving you opportunity to share your story)

Name:_____

Address:_____

City/State/Zip _____

Telephone: _____Home

_____Cell

E-Mail: _____

Please return this form to: Concepts of Truth International
P. O. Box 1438
Wynne, AR 72396
Phone: 870.238.4329

References

(n.d.). Retrieved April 14, 2011, from http://www.oxytocin.org/oxytoc/love-science.html.

Anne Stevens, M. P. (2002). Maternal and Fetal Microchimerism: Implications for Human Diseases. *American Academy of Pediatrics*.

Concepts of Truth, Inc. (n.d.). Retrieved January 15, 2011, from International Helpline for Abortion Recovery and Prevention: http://www.nationalhelpline.org

Davis, L. M. (2009). Artist, www.lynnemariedavis.com. *Jesus Delivers*. Gainsville, Georgia: Concepts of Truth Inc.

Demoss, N. L. (n.d.). *reviveourhearts.com*. Retrieved February 14, 2011, from reviveourhearts.com: http://www.reviveourhearts.com/pdf/uploads/TheHeartGodRevives.pdf

Dictionary, M. -W. (n.d.). *Merriam-Webster Online Dictionary*. Retrieved February 5, 2011, from Merriam-Webster Online Dictionary: http://www.merriam-webster.com

Ellis, A. (n.d.). *albertellisinfo.com*. Retrieved February 14, 2011, from albertellisinfo.com: http://www.rebt.ws/REBT%20explained.htm

Family, F. o. (n.d.). *downloads/Heartlink*. Retrieved February 14, 2011, from focusonthefamily.com: http://www.focusonthefamily.com/downloads/heartlink/pdf/firstninemonthsbook.pdf

Koerbel, L. F. (1997). *Fitting the Pieces Together*. Atoka, TN: Post Abortion Ministries (P-A-M).

Kubler-Ross, E. (1969). *On Death and Dying*. Simon & Schuster.

Lang, B. (n.d.). *The Bible Study*. Retrieved from bibletopics.com: http://www.bibletopics.com

Lucado, M. (1995). *The Inspirational Study Bible*. Word Publishing.

McGee, T. S. (1990 2nd Edition). *Search for Significance*. Houston, TX: Rapha Publishing.

Names, B. B. (n.d.). *biblical-baby-names.com*. Retrieved February 12, 2011, from biblical-baby-names.com: http://www.biblical-baby-names.com

Philosophy, I. E. (n.d.). *Origen of Alexandria*. Retrieved February 13, 2011, from Internet Encyclopedia of Philosophy: http://www.iep.utm.edu/origen-of-alexandria/

Piper, J. (2009). American Association of Christian Counselors. *The Praise of the Glory of His Grace*. Nashville, TN: AACC.net.

Pleasant White, P. (n.d.). *Legend of the Tear Jar*. Retrieved September 2008, from webhealing.com: http://www.webhealing.com/articles/tearjar1.htm

Smith, H. E. Love Lifted Me. *Heavenly Highways Songbook*. Brentwood - Benson Music Publishing, Nashville, TN.

Terry Selby, M. A. (n.d.). Abortive Woman's Thinking System. Wynne, AR: Concepts of Truth Inc. modified to include men.

The Names of God Series. (n.d.). Retrieved February 14, 2011, from preceptaustin.org: http://www. preceptaustin.org

Bev McGraw, MSE **
Magnolia Pines
901 S. Cleveland
Wynne, AR 72396
870-238-6300

Odell McCallum, MSE **
First National Bank
1714 Oakdale Lane
Wynne, AR 72396
870-238-8904
870-238-2361 work

George Conner III, MD **
Forrest City Family Medical
260 SFC 471
Forrest City, AR 72335
870-633-1351
870-633-1256 work

Diane Pagan**
PO Box 385
Wynne, AR 72396
870-588-1280

Bill Morgan**
19 CR 715
Wynne, AR 72396
870-238-3690

Father Ed Graves *
St. Peters Catholic Church
P O Box 517
Wynne, AR 72396
870-238-2613

Dr. Matt Pearson
Eldorado First Baptist Church
2106 West Oak
Eldorado, AR 71730
870-814-9924

Pastor Tom Sawyer
Middle Sandy EPC
PO Box 153
Homeworth, OH 44634
330-525-7840

Dr. Thomas Lindberg
First Assembly of God
8914 River Meadow Drive
Cordova, TN 38018
901-843-8600

Esther Witcher, CPA
PO Box 306
Wynne, AR 72396
870-238-3245

Dr. Jared Pingleton, Psy. D., Director
Counseling Services
Focus on the Family
8605 Explorer Drive
Colorado Springs, CO 80995

Father Frank Pavone
Priest for Life
PO Box 141172
Staten Island, NY 10314
1-888-PFL-3448

Dr. Rex Horne, Jr., President
Ouachita Baptist University
410 Ouachita St.
Arkadelphia, AR 71998
1-870-245-5000

Bishop Anthony B. Taylor
Diocese of Little Rock
2500 North Tyler St
PO Box 7565
Little Rock, AR 72217
501-664-0340

Peggy Hartshorn, Ph.D., President
Heartbeat International
665 E. Dublin-Granville Rd. Suite 440
Columbus, OH 43229
614-885-7577

**Concepts of Truth International
   Board Members
 *Advisory Board Member

What People are Saying . . .

"Concepts focuses on the sanctity of life from the womb to the tomb. So many lives have been transformed through this ministry and I'm so thankful to be a part of it." Pastor Rusty Blann, First Assembly of God, West Memphis, AR

"What rises to the top for me, personally, about what I love about Concepts of Truth is their commitment to the Gospel of Jesus Christ. That is central in everything they do." Dr. Matt Pearson, Wynne Baptist Church, Wynne, AR

"Concepts of Truth is such an important blessing for the church today. Our nation continues to live in denial, as if no harm has occurred from abortion, but there are millions of hurting people all around us and in our congregations. I worked through the healing process without many resources with one of my church members who is now on the national counseling hotline. Concepts of Truth's resources make the healing process so much easier." Pastor Tom Sawyer, Middle Sandy Evangelical Presbyterian Church, Homeworth, OH

"If a person is experiencing confusion, pain, or suffering after an abortion, what a blessing to be able to be connected 24/7 to a person who once felt the same but has experienced healing and can now provide hope and practical help to others. This is only possible through the International Helpline for Abortion Recovery and Prevention." Peggy Hartshorn, Ph.D., President, Heartbeat International, Columbus, OH

"I commend you for your work and support of life issues. Life is a great miracle in all its forms, and a wonderful blessing where God's love is visible to all of us. I am happy to endorse the work that you do." Anthony B. Taylor, Bishop, Diocese of Little Rock, Little Rock, AR

Concepts of Recovery The Journey Group Weekend Schedule

FRIDAY

3:00 pm	**Registration**/*Settle In Rooms*
3:30-5:30 pm	**Orientation, Ground Rules, Sharing Stories &** **Discussion** *Chapter 1 Where Am I?*
5:30-6:30 pm	**Dinner**
6:30-8:00 pm	**Discussion** *Chapter 2 The Map Maker*
8:00-8:30 pm	**Dessert**
8:30-10:00 pm	**Study Chapter** *3 Traveling Companions Relief & Denial*

SATURDAY

7:30-8:30 am	**Breakfast**
8:30-10:00 am	**Discussion** *Chapter 3 Traveling Companions Relief & Denial*
10:00-12:00 Noon	**Study** *Chapter 4 Roadblock of Anger*
12:00-1:00 pm	**Lunch**
1:00-2:30 pm	**Discussion** *Chapter 4 Roadblock of Anger*
2:30-3:30 pm	**Study** *Chapter 5 Taking Forgiveness by the Hand*
3:30-5:30 pm	**Discussion** *Chapter 5 Taking Forgiveness by the Hand*
5:30-6:30 pm	**Dinner**
6:30-7:30 pm	**Study** *Chapter 6 Valley of Depression*
7:30-8:00 pm	**Dessert**
8:00-8:30 pm	**Preparation for Art Workshop**
8:30-10:00 pm	**Discussion** *Chapter 6 Valley of Depression & Tilly DVD*

SUNDAY

7:30-8:00 am	**Breakfast**
8:00-9:00 am	**Study** *Chapter 7 Carried by God's Grace*
9:00-10:00 am	**Discussion** *Chapter 7 Carried by God's Grace*
10:00-11:00 am	**Study** *Chapter 8 Letting Go*
11:00-12:30 pm	**Discussion** *Chapter 8 Letting Go and Art Workshop*
12:30-2:00 pm	**Lunch, Rest & Dress** for Memorial Service
2:00-3:00 pm	**Memorial Service**
3:00-4:00 pm	**Dessert Reception, Evaluations & Departure**

Note: Assign Chapter 9 for a follow-up conference call or local group meeting two weeks after completing the weekend. For weekend schedule, participants need to complete Chapters 1 and 2 before this schedule begins. For weekly schedule, groups meet for nine weeks plus Memorial Service. Discussion time will be in the Group. Study time is in personal room.

Concepts of Recovery The Journey Evaluation Sheet

Date_____   Please circle M for male or F for female: M   F

Place _____
Group Facilitator's Name _____
Co- Facilitator's Name _____
Observer/Trainee's Name _____

Please write an **overall summary** of your retreat weekend experience. If you give us permission to use your comments, initial here _____.

Rate the Program. Put an X in the box under your choice for each comment.

	Fair	Good	Excellent
1. Upon completing the weekend, I received the help in the major problem areas that I had stated in my goals for the weekend.			
2. After completing *Concepts of Recovery The Journey*, I would recommend the program to others.			
3. I understand more about my needs in abortion recovery after completing this program.			

Rate the Facilitators. Put an X in the box under your choice for each comment.

	Fair	Good	Excellent
1. Facilitators were knowledgeable about the subject area.			
2. Facilitators shared the information in an understandable manner.			
3. Facilitators had a caring attitude toward the group.			

©2011 Concepts of Truth International

About the Author & Founder of Concepts of Truth

First of all, the Author is Jesus Christ! He birthed Concepts of Truth in my (Millie's) heart after an 8 yr. old little boy could not learn John 1:1. Because of a passion to teach children to know the Word of God, Concepts of Truth was born!

It was 1997. I had been working for several years on getting some questions put to music for Junior Bible Quiz, and the cassette tape was being produced. I remember standing around our computer in the dining area of our house with my husband and sons as we brainstormed a name for the ministry. The tape being produced was called "*Buzzing Melodies*" but that didn't sound like the right name for the entire ministry. After several hours of discussion around the word "truth," my oldest son asked, "what about Concepts of Truth?" and immediately we all loved it! Since the ministry was founded on the Word of God, we felt we had chosen the perfect name. We began to research and found that there was no other Concepts of Truth in Arkansas so we decided to apply for the trademark name. So Concepts of Truth incorporated in March 1998 beginning as a small tape ministry for Junior Bible Quiz and opened as a professional counseling and pregnancy care center in 2001. Our purpose is to promote the gospel of Jesus Christ by all means and forms possible, including but not limited to, providing an International Helpline for Abortion Recovery and Prevention, counseling, singing, teaching, personal testimonies, tape & video productions. ***Our vision is for the world to know God's truth and make healthy life choices. Our mission is to share God's truth about life around the world providing counseling services and a model for sexual health, educating in abortion recovery and prevention to equip the whole person to make healthy life choices & empower future generations.*** Concepts of Truth, Inc is an international, faith-based, 501 C-3, non profit organization providing counseling, recovery and prevention making a difference in people's lives.

We provide professional counseling on a sliding scale based on income and need, sexual health classes in the public schools, and the International Helpline for Abortion Recovery and Prevention at 866.482.LIFE. The International Helpline for Abortion Recovery and Prevention is an integral part of the mission of Concepts of Truth because of the great untouched mission field of those hurting after abortion. All calls are free and confidential. The number is used as a resource on the *Faces of Abortion* TV Show and documentaries. It is also referenced in many books, brochures and websites for abortion recovery resources. The International Helpline for Abortion Recovery and Prevention is more than a referral source. We provide callers with referrals to abortion recovery help centers all over the world, mail resources, and provide on-going follow up and support until the caller has processed the pain and grief of abortion and healed to be able to help others.

The International Helpline for Abortion Recovery and Prevention has served callers from all 50 states, Canada, Puerto Rico, Europe, Dubai and Japan. Callers are given life affirming options enhancing their vision and value to empower them to make choices for life. These life choices include saving the unborn, healing after abortion, adoption placement, and new and renewed spiritual life.

> " *Any country that accepts abortion is the poorest of the poor.* "
>
> ~ *Mother Teresa*

CPSIA information can be obtained
at www.ICGtesting.com
Printed in the USA
BVHW021137011121
620455BV00015B/267